Caroline Feller Bauer's

Leading Kids
to Books
through

CRAFTS

Illustrated by

Richard Laurent

AMERICAN LIBRARY ASSOCIATION
Chicago and London
2000

Project editor: Bradley Hannan

Text and cover design by Dianne M. Rooney

Composition by Dianne Rooney in Bembo and Tekton using QuarkXpress 4.04 for the Macintosh

Printed on 50-pound white offset, a pH-neutral stock, and bound in 10-point coated cover stock by McNaughton & Gunn

The paper used in this publication meets the minimum requirements of American National Standard for Information Sciences—Permanence of Paper for Printed Library Materials, ANSI Z39.48-1992. ∞

Library of Congress Cataloging-in-Publication Data

Bauer, Caroline Feller.
    Leading kids to books through crafts / Caroline Feller Bauer.
        p.   cm. — (Mighty easy motivator series)
    ISBN 0-8389-0769-5 (alk. paper)
    1. Children's libraries—Activity programs—United States. 2. Book talks—United States. 3. Creative activities and seat work. 4. Handicraft—United States. 5. Children's literature—Bibliography. I. Title. II. Series: Bauer, Caroline Feller. Mighty easy motivators.
    Z718.2.U6B38   1999
    027.62'5—dc21   99-41387

04   03   02   5   4   3   2

*For the Ladies' Craft Group
of Chittagong, Bangladesh,
with apologies for talking
about Noah
instead of crafting.*

Small Craft Warning!

Charles Ghigna

I'd like to make a gift for Mom
To give to her today,
But every time I do a craft
My hands get in the way.

I think of lots of things to make
But sometimes I get stuck.
The only time it turns out right
Is with a lot of luck.

The next time that I make a craft
My hands will hold on tight
Around a book on crafts until—
I *read* to get it right!

Contents

Contents

Acknowledgments

Every effort has been made to trace the ownership of all copyrighted material within and to secure the necessary permissions to reprint these selections. In the event of any question arising as to the use of any material, the editor and publisher, while expressing regret for any inadvertent error, will be happy to make the necessary correction in future printings.

Grateful acknowledgment is made to the following for permission to reprint the copyrighted material listed below:

"Small Craft Warning!" Copyright © 1999 by Charles Ghigna (aka "Father Goose").

"At The Zoo" by A.A. Milne. Illustrations by E. H. Shepard, from WHEN WE WERE VERY YOUNG by A.A. Milne, illustrations by E. H. Shepard. Copyright 1924 by E. P. Dutton, renewed 1952 by A.A. Milne. Used by permission of Dutton Children's Books, a division of Penguin Putnam Inc.

"The Thing." Copyright © 1999 by Charles Ghigna (aka "Father Goose").

"Just for Fun," by Beverly McLoughland from *Humpty Dumpty's Magazine,* copyright © 1976 Parents Magazine Enterprises. Used by permission of Children's Better Health Institute, Benjamin Franklin Literary & Medical Society, Inc., Indianapolis, Indiana.

Acknowledgments

"Blowing Bubbles" from *Stilts, Somersaults, and Headstands* by Kathleen Fraser. Copyright 1968 by Kathleen Fraser. Reprinted by permission of Curtis Brown, Ltd.

Text excerpt from *Harry's Birthday,* text copyright © BY BARBARA ANN PORTE. Used by permission of HarperCollins Publisher.

"Elevator," from *Roomrimes,* by Sylvia Cassedy (Thomas Y. Crowell Co., 1987, © Sylvia Cassedy). Reprinted by permission of Ellen Cassedy.

"Too Many Daves" from THE SNEETCHES AND OTHER STORIES by Dr. Seuss. TM and copyright © 1961 and copyright renewed 1989 by Dr. Seuss Enterprises, L. P. Reprinted by permission of Random House, Inc.

Yung-Kyung-Pyung from *Anansi, the Spider Man: Jamaican Folk Tales,* told by Philip M. Sherlock, published by Thomas Y. Crowell, 1954. Copyright 1954 by Philip M. Sherlock.

"Lucky Ladybugs!" Copyright © 1999 by Charles Ghigna (aka "Father Goose").

"Round and Round" by Mary Ann Hoberman reprinted by permission of Gina Maccoby Literary Agency © 1991 by Mary Ann Hoberman.

"Living in W'ales" by Richard Hughes from *The Spider's Palace,* published by Random House, copyright 1960.

"I Brought a Worm" reprinted with the permission of Simon & Schuster Books for Young Readers, an imprint of Simon & Schuster Children's Publishing Division from IF YOU'RE NOT HERE, PLEASE RAISE YOUR HAND by Kalli Dakos. Text copyright © 1990 Kalli Dakos.

"Why I'm Glad I'm Not a Worm," from THE OTHER SIDE OF THE DOOR by Jeff Moss. Copyright © 1991 by Jeff Moss. Used by permission of Bantam Books, a division of Random House, Inc.

"Two Gardeners" from BING BANG BOING, copyright © 1994 by Douglas Florian, reprinted by permission of Harcourt, Inc.

Acknowledgments

"The Worm Song" Text copyright © 1993 by Brod Bagert from *Chicken Socks and Other Contagious Poems* by Brod Bagert. Published by Boyds Mills Press, Inc. Reprinted with permission.

"A Crafty Idea!" Copyright © 1999 by Charles Ghigna (aka "Father Goose").

The Crafty Road
to Books

I was a lucky kid! My bedroom had a door leading up a staircase that ended in an attic everyone called "Caroline's Playroom." The attic was mine, all mine. No one ever said it was messy or that I had to clean it up. I saved everything up there: buttons, little bottles, bus transfers, string, ribbon, parts of old clocks, and anything remotely useful for making something out of something else. I was devoted to designing clothes for paper dolls. I carved animals from Ivory soap and cut designs on potato halves. In those days, no one put warning labels on craft boxes or thought to warn children not to cut anything by themselves. I could make up craft projects just for the joy of creating.

Then I was a lucky mother! When my daughter Hilary was a little girl, our family lived on a street that seemed to have no children. One day, I spied a young woman walking with a toddler. They entered the house at the end of our street. A playmate! I thought. How to meet them? Simple. I rang the bell and as my friend Joni, the little girl's mother, is fond of relating, I said, "Hi. My name is Caroline. I have a three-year-old, so we have to be friends."

It rains a lot in Oregon, so Joni and I spent much of our time inside while the girls got into mischief. To occupy ourselves, Joni and I made crafts. Since I had taken a decoupage class, we decoupaged everything: the walls, furniture, blocks. The house smelled of varnish. There were scraps of paper all over the kitchen floor.

Joni and I moved on to painting eggs. We ate endless amounts of scrambled eggs and omelettes after we blew out the insides of the eggs. After eggs, we thought of a thousand things to do with empty tennis ball cans and cardboard tubes. Luckily, summer arrived and we could go outside and play tennis with the balls from the cans we had pirated.

Joni and I became the neighborhood Craft Queens. Whenever anyone was looking for a craft to entertain children at a birthday party or school program, we were available for consultation, ideas, and help. We knew crafts were fun and wanted to share what we had learned.

Later, as a children's librarian in public libraries and schools, I incorporated crafts into my book programs. I quickly discovered how much children enjoy learning with crafts. The best part of hands-on projects is that kids rarely think of themselves as learning; they merely enjoy keeping busy making a finished product they can treasure. Colors, shapes, textures, all play a part in enticing children to create something that enhances whatever story or poem I present. Engaging the mind and body—as with a story and accompanying craft—leaves a more lasting impression on youngsters.

Think of the many ways crafts can enhance your literature program. Crafts can:

- introduce characters
- focus attention on the story and author
- display scenes
- explain action or plot
- recap story highlights
- emphasize a main theme
- increase language development

- improve general eye–hand coordination that stimulates learning
- reinforce the story's message

How Leading Kids to Books through Crafts Works

Through the years I have discovered that there are probably no new crafts, just variations of existing ones. Therefore, many crafts in this book may seem familiar to you. Now you can offer them to a whole new generation of children, so they can create their own variations.

I have also found that most group leaders, whether in libraries, classrooms, or recreation centers, are short on time for preparation and the programs themselves. This book, number three in the Mighty Easy Motivators series, presents ideas for book programs that introduce children to the wonders of books while giving them the opportunity to make quick and inexpensive take-home souvenirs—reminders of the literature they experienced.

I know you will adapt these suggestions to your own situation. The material is meant to be a springboard, inspiring you to bring children and books together through crafts. As in my earlier books, I once again urge you to:

Think Simple.

Think Creative.

Think Fun.

And always . . . Think Books.

The Program

Each suggested program has two objectives. One is to introduce children to exciting new stories and poems. The other is to help boys and girls create a story-related craft to take home. For this, parents of participants will love you. Finally, they will have an answer to the question, "What did you do at the library?" Most children who answer "nothing" will now have something to show.

Stories, Books, and Poems to Share

Stories or poems accompany many of the crafts, and you can use them right from the book. You will also find a list of additional titles after each craft. The books listed with these activities were chosen because they are particularly appropriate for the theme. They either fit the theme directly or extend it. Introduce a variety of the stories before each craft, and encourage the children to read the books another time. If possible, display the books for days afterward as a reminder.

If you do not have access to these particular titles, don't panic. They are meant to be a guide. Undoubtedly, you can find other titles to add to the list that will work just as well. Choose one and share it with your group. Booktalk the others, and exhibit them during and after the program.

Crafts

All crafts have been tested with children—and on anyone else who happened to be in the vicinity when I was presenting them. I tried to keep the directions easy to follow. A visual rendering accompanies the directions in the text to help with those items that are difficult to visualize.

Most of the crafts can be made in less than fifteen minutes, if the materials are on hand. This does not include cleanup, however, or monitoring a group of enthusiastic children. I do recommend planning ahead for projects, that is, gathering the materials and placing them in order of use before the program begins. Advance planning gives you less to think about should your program include a group of wiggleworms.

I also recommend preparing a sample of each craft before you present it to the group. That way, you are more comfortable with the project and can plan alternatives for preparation steps you think may be too difficult or too easy for a given group.

The materials are easy-to-obtain art supplies, such as construction or computer paper. You probably have most of the materials in your library or classroom. In many cases, you will need to provide enough scissors for everyone to use or share. You may want to invest in boxes of blunt-point scissors, if they are not in your cabinet already.

In the Supplies list you will occasionally find the phrase "art materials of your choice." This means that you can select from crayons, felt-tip markers, colored pencils, paints, or whatever you have collected in your art cupboard or choose to purchase. Sometimes the choice boils down to available time, size of the group, or age of the children. For one program, paints may be too ambitious a choice for a half-hour project with 30 preschoolers and minimal adult assistance. In another situation, you may find that advance preparation of some steps toward the completed item will work best. Then if you are pressed for time, the children can merely color and assemble.

Try to remember that the children should try their own ideas whenever possible and not just follow the lines. The more latitude you give children toward preparing a project the more satisfied they will be to bring home something they made at the library.

Some leaders prefer to organize the art supplies at each child's place at a table. If time permits, however, I prefer for children to participate in the preparation, including passing out supplies. Involvement in preparation gives the children a sense of the project from start to finish. Remember that it is not the end product you strive for but the fun of creating.

There are so many great crafts that I had difficulty limiting what to include in this book. Several crafts didn't fit with a single topic, so I added a section called General Crafts. You can use the projects in this section with any story or book you prefer. For example, the section Sculpt a Book Character gives three different homemade clay recipes for sculpting favorite characters or scenes. Other crafts focus on the wonder of reading without a more specific theme. These projects provide an avenue for children to express their joy in stories, books, poems, and their connections to crafts.

Whichever crafts and stories you choose, remember to have fun with the presentation. Crafts and literature go together naturally, blending information to promote the love of books and reading. Therefore, join me on the crafty road to books. I had a perfectly splendid time traveling the road, playing with these crafts. I hope you and the children you work with will, too.

Animal Pendants

Animal crackers and A. A. Milne. What a treat! This poem about animals is fun, and the craft is good enough to eat. In fact, girls and boys will like doing just that, so buy extra crackers.

Read the poem to your group. Talk about the different animals—real or otherwise—they hear about in the poem. Invite listeners to make a pendant of their favorite animal for a necklace.

Craft an Animal Cracker Pendant

Supplies

animal crackers (at least two per child: one to craft and one to eat)

permanent ink felt-tip pens

white glue

small paper clips (one for each pendant)

yarn or string

scissors

masking tape

Preparation

Give an animal cracker to each participant or let children choose their own. Have them color their animal with a felt-tip pen and outline the main parts in black (1). Tell kids to use the raised portions on the animal as their guide where to color the black.

Direct the artists to spread white glue on the colored side of the animal. Let the glue dry while you share an animal book. Then ask children to glue the back of the animal. This makes the cracker stronger.

Before the glue on the backside dries, tell participants to wrap a piece of masking tape around half the paper clip (2). Glue the masking tape end to the back of the cracker (3). The other end should stick out above the cracker, forming a loop.

Cut pieces of yarn or string long enough for children to wear around their necks. Help children pass a piece of yarn or string through the loop on their cracker and tie the ends together (4). Watch the smiles as they slip the necklace over their head.

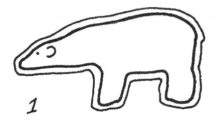

1

2   *3 and 4*

Share a Poem

At the Zoo

A. A. Milne

There are lions and roaring tigers, and enormous camels
and things,

There are biffalo-buffalo-
bisons, and a great
big bear with wings,
There's a sort of a tiny
potamus, and a tiny
nosserustoo—
But *I* gave buns to the elephant when *I* went down to
the Zoo!

There are badgers and bidgers and bodgers, and a
Superintendent's House,
There are masses of goats, and a Polar, and different
kinds of mouse,
And I think there's a sort of a something which is called
a wallaboo—
But *I* gave buns to the elephant when *I* went down to
the Zoo!

If you try to talk to the bison, he never quite under-
stands;
You can't shake hands with a mingo—he doesn't like
shaking hands.
And lions and roaring tigers hate saying, "How do you
do?" —
But *I* give buns to the elephant when
I go down to the Zoo!

Share a Book

Animals

Alborough, Jez. *Watch Out! Big Bro's Coming!* Art by the author. Candlewick, 1997. A little mouse warns the jungle animals of the approach of big Bro, who turns out to be the mouse's big brother.

Gelman, Rita Golden. *I Went to the Zoo.* Art by Maryann Kovalski. Scholastic, 1993. A boy takes all the zoo animals home with him.

Hazelaar, Cor. *Zoo Dreams.* Art by the author. Farrar, Strauss, 1997. A night-time visit to the zoo.

Micklethwait, Lucy. *I Spy a Lion: Animals in Art.* Illustrated with fine art. Greenwillow, 1994. Find the animals in the work of famous artists.

Morris, Desmond. *The World of Animals.* Art by Peter Barrett. Viking, 1993. Two- or three-page essays and drawings of 24 animals.

Pandell, Karen. *Animal Action ABC.* Photos by Art Wolfe and Nancy Sheehan. Dutton, 1996. Action photos of children and animals.

Paul, Anthony. *The Tiger Who Lost His Stripes.* Art by Michael Foreman. Harcourt, 1995. General Mac-Tiger searches the jungle for his lost stripes.

West, Colin. *One Day in the Jungle.* Candlewick, 1995. Each animal sneezes louder than the one before until the elephant sneezes the jungle away.

Books

W hat fun for kids to make their own books after hearing Charles Ghigna's delightful poem! Either of these two types of paper books will do.

Possible subjects for the books? The elephant and bird from the poem, of course. Or perhaps your children prefer to select their own topics. Still need subjects? Here are some ideas to suggest:

- the family—each page could be a different family member, including pets
- home/neighborhood
- a typical day/school day
- holidays
- animals
- favorite sports or activities
- how to do something
- retelling another story/fairy tale/book/poem
- an illustrated letter to a friend or relative, describing a birthday party or other special event
- favorite quotes from other sources

Craft a Stairstep Book

Supplies

5 sheets of 8-1/2" x 11" paper
stapler

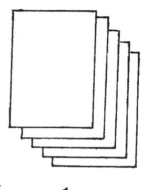

1

Preparation

Lay one sheet of paper on a flat surface. Layer the pages by placing the next sheet 1/2" below the top edge of the first sheet. Lay the next sheet 1/2" below the top of the second sheet. Continue layering by placing each of the five sheets 1/2" below the top of the sheet under it (1). Reduce the number of pages if you have limited time or are working with younger children.

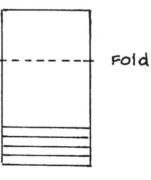

Fold

Now fold all the pages over from the edge nearest you. The bottom of the top sheet (edge nearest you) should fold to 1/2" below the top edge (farthest from you) of the same sheet. Press down the crease of the five sheets (2). Turn the folded edge to the top away from you, and you will see a series of layered pages (3).

2

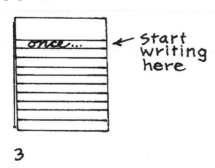

start
writing
here

3

4

If you used five sheets of paper, you now have ten pages for writing and drawing a story. Start your story on the top layer. Write the text of the story on the 1/2" space (4). There is room to draw an illustration on each page under the flap, adding an element of surprise. To ensure the layers stay in place, staple them at the fold.

Craft an 8-Page Miniature Book

Supplies

one sheet of 8-1/2" x 11" paper

scissors

art materials of your choice

Preparation

Fold the paper in half lengthwise. Match the two short edges and fold in half again to look like a greeting card. Match the two short edges again and fold the paper in half.

Then unfold the entire sheet. Again fold the page in half, this time width-wise. Place the four-section folded paper before you. Cut or tear down along the center crease from the folded edge to the halfway point. Reopen the paper and fold again lengthwise. Gently push the end sections together until they fold into a small book. You will have eight pages to fill, counting the outer covers. Staple along the inside fold, if you wish.

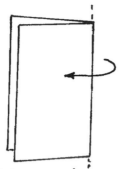

1. Fold paper in half lengthwise.

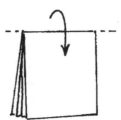

2. Fold in half again, as for a book or a greeting card.

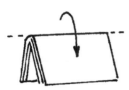

3. Fold in half again.

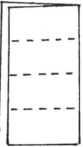

4. Unfold the sheet and fold in half width-wise.

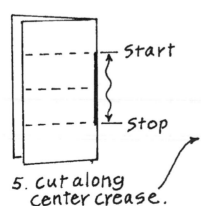

Start

Stop

5. Cut along center crease.

Hint: Fold in half <u>width-wise</u>. Cut along center crease from the folded edge to the half way point.

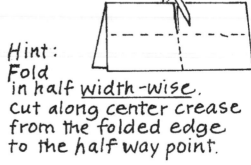

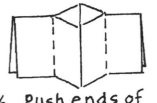

6. Push ends of paper together.

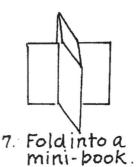

7. Fold into a mini-book.

8. Staple if you wish.

Share a Poem

The Thing

Charles Ghigna

I got a lot of paper.
I got a lot of string.
I tied it all together
And made a special thing.

I got a lot of markers.
I wrote a lot of words.
I drew a lot of pictures
Of elephants and birds.
I showed it to my neighbor.
I showed it to my dad.

But no one ever figured out
Exactly what I had.

I showed it to the baby.
I let her have a look.
She chewed upon the pages—
She knew it was a book!

Share a Book

Writing

Brown, Marc. *Arthur Writes a Story.* Art by the author. Little, 1996. Arthur writes a story for his homework assignment.

Christelow, Eileen. *What Do Authors Do?* Art by the author. Clarion, 1995. Two authors create entirely different books about their pets.

Kehoe, Michael. *A Book Takes Root: The Making of a Picture Book.* Art by the author. Carolrhoda, 1993. A photo essay following the creation of a picture book from start to finish.

Krensky, Stephen. *Breaking into Print: Before and After the Invention of the Printing Press.* Art by Bonnie Christensen. Little, 1996. A history of bookmaking from the 1400s to the present.

Lester, Helen. *Author: A True Story.* Art by the author. Houghton, 1997. In a sprightly picture book, Lester shows a little girl at three and as an adult, writing.

Stevens, Janet. *From Pictures to Words.* Art by the author. Holiday, 1995. An illustrator takes the reader through the steps of creating a book with the animals of her imagination.

Elephants

Blumberg, Rhoda. *Jumbo*. Art by Jonathan Hunt. Bradbury, 1992. The story of the famous circus elephant.

De Vries, Anke. *My Elephant Can Do Anything*. Art by Ilja Walraven. Front Street, 1995. An acrobatic elephant balances on a coffeepot and accomplishes other astounding feats.

Farris, Pamela J. *Young Mouse and Elephant: An East African Folktale*. Art by Valeri Gorbachev. Houghton, 1996. Mouse brags that he is the strongest animal.

Rovetch, Lissa. *Cora and the Elephants*. Art by Lissa Rovetch and Martha Weston. Viking, 1995. Cora lives with a family of elephants in Africa, but where is her real family?

Birds

Carlstrom, Nancy White. *Raven and River*. Art by Jon Van Zyle. Little Brown, 1997. Raven flies over Alaska, awakening the arctic animals.

Kamal, Aleph. *The Bird Who Was an Elephant*. Art by Frane Lessac. Harper, 1990. A bird visits a village in India.

Keller, Holly. *Grandfather's Dream*. Art by the author. Greenwillow, 1994. A grandfather in Vietnam hopes the cranes will return to his war-torn country.

Torres, Leyla. *Subway Sparrow*. Art by the author. Farrar, Srauss, 1993. Four people in a New York subway train try to capture a trapped sparrow.

Williams, Suzanne. *Library Lil*. Art by Steven Kellogg. Dial, 1997. Strong-willed Library Lil encourages the whole town to use the library.

Bubbles

Just try bubbles
once, and you and
your children will want to do
it again. Bubbles are fun, inexpensive, and magical. They are a
natural fit as a craft activity for this poem. Try not to
worry about the potential mess. Bubbles are just soap
and water. The whole mirage disappears when the bubbles burst.

Supplies

6 cups of water (distilled water, if possible)
2 cups of liquid detergent (Joy or Dawn works best)
3/4 cups of light corn syrup *or* 1 cup glycerin (available
    at drugstores)
bucket or tub to hold liquids
paper towels/sponges (just in case you have spills)
bubble wands *(See* Preparation)

Preparation

Before preparing this activity, collect as many objects as
you can with openings to dip into your liquid soap mix-

ture. Test how well they form a suitable wand with a handle. Experiment with different shapes. Bubble wands can be made from:

pipe cleaners (available in craft shops)

wire coat hangers

yarn attached through two straws

macrame rings

embroidery hoops

kitchen utensils with holes, such
    as strainers or slotted spoons

To mix the bubbles, gently stir the liquid ingredients in a bucket or tub. The best bubbles come from mixtures left for several hours or overnight in a covered container. The mixture works better when it is left alone before using, rather than stirred, which creates surface bubbles.

To begin the activity, give each child a bubble wand. If you have wands made from different materials or formed into different shapes, encourage experimenting. You can give each child a cup filled halfway with bubble liquid or direct students to share one or more containers. Either way, be sure to set up a few rules with the children for your bubble extravaganza:

- One person in the bucket at a time, if children share containers.
- Only blow bubbles away from the furniture.
- Never blow bubbles in someone's face.

You can have bubble-blowing contests for biggest, smallest, longest-living, and most unusual bubble.

I prefer, however, to plan a program of old-fashioned unstructured time to experiment with the small miracle of bubbles.

Share a Poem

Just for Fun
Beverly McLoughland

I blew a bubble
Round and slow,
But just before
I let it go,
I saw it catch
A bit of sun,
And make a rainbow
Just for fun.

Blowing Bubbles
Kathleen Fraser

Bubbles are big enough
to see your face in
or a real rainbow
and small enough to get lost
almost as fast as they arrive.
How sad . . .
But look! Here comes a new one.

Share a Book

Bubbles

Durant, Penny Raife. *Bubblemania!* Art by Gary Mohrman. Avon, 1994. Experiments with bubbles.

O'Connor, Jane. *Benny's Big Bubble.* Art by Tomie dePaola. Grosset, 1997. Rebus pictures and simple words that show a bubble on its voyage.

Zubrowski, Bernie. *A Children's Museum Activity Book: Bubbles.* Art by Joan Drescher. Little, 1979. Activities with bubbles.

Coyote and Rabbit

I n the United States, we enjoy coyote stories from other cultures. You will find many coyote stories in picture books and anthologies presented for children and adults. Although the coyote is usually considered a trickster, he is often the animal who gets tricked. In some stories, the rabbit turns into the victor.

Craft a Parade of Rabbit and His Relatives

Supplies

newspaper or newsprint (Wrapping paper also works well, since it is colorful and light enough to cut through.)

construction, card, banner, or other heavier paper

scissors

pencils

Preparation

Precut an appropriate number of rabbit designs on heavier paper. To prepare your sample, open a sheet of newspaper and cut a strip 5" high and the width of the two-page newspaper spread (1). These, too, can be precut to save time in your program. Accordion pleat the paper strip (2). Trace or outline the heavier paper rabbit design (3). See illustration. Cut out rabbit chain (4).

During the activity encourage children to experiment with their own designs and other size rabbits. You can also use my favorite art supply, a sheet of stiffer paper. Cut the paper in half lengthwise and fold accordion style. Outline and cut the rabbits as with the newspaper. Rabbits cut from stiffer paper will probably come out smaller, but rabbits are small. If time permits, children can cut several strips and glue the ends together, forming a longer rabbit parade.

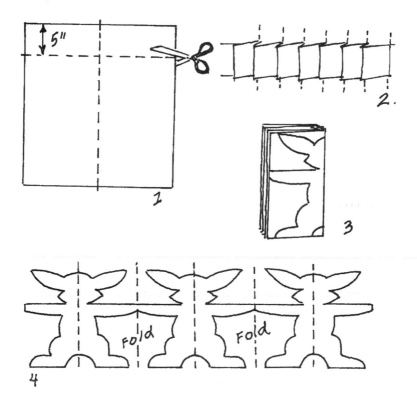

Craft a Circle of Coyotes

Supplies

sheet of 8-1/2" x 11" paper (or 8" square sheet
of paper)

scissors

pencil

Preparation

Fold the bottom edge of the paper until it lines up with
the left-hand edge, forming a triangle with the folded section. Cut off the top unfolded portion of the paper, creating an 8" square sheet. With the square still folded, match
the points on either end of the creased (longest edge of
triangle) side and fold. Match the corners from the longest
edge once again and fold. When you open the square, you
should see eight triangle sections (1).

Place the square on one point, so it looks like a diamond. Refold the diamond until you have one triangle
(2). Copy the coyote pattern with its back along the fold
(3), or design your own pattern. Cut along the lines and
open gently to reveal a circle of coyotes. Add features if
you like.

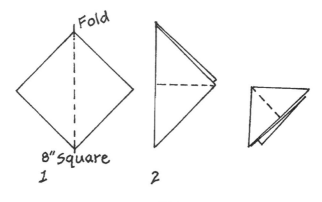

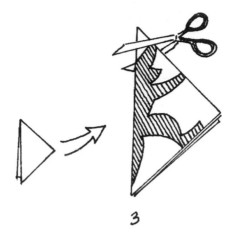

3

Share a Story

Rabbit Wins

Caroline Feller Bauer

Coyote was looking forward to a good dinner. He was sure that this time he could capture Rabbit. To trap Rabbit, Coyote hid behind a rock just at the lip of the cliff.

Pretty soon, along came Rabbit. Hop! Hop! Hop!

Coyote leaped out in front of Rabbit. "Good morning, friend Rabbit," Coyote greeted him with a smile.

"And a good morning to you, Coyote," Rabbit said, ready to run for his life. But as Rabbit quickly searched for an escape path, he realized that no direction seemed safe.

Coyote delighted to see Rabbit's eyes dart from side to side and a worried look slowly creep over

his face. "I'm happy that you
walked by this rock, my friend,"
Coyote said licking his lips. "You see,
there is no way for you to escape. If you
walk away from me, you will fall off the
cliff. You have no choice but to hop
directly to me. You are cornered."

Poor Rabbit. He was too small to fight
Coyote. Besides Rabbit never liked to
fight. Even if he could get past
Coyote, Rabbit would surely tire
before Coyote caught him. Coyote could
run forever. Rabbit wondered how he
could escape. Suddenly he brightened.

"Dear Coyote, although you have
me cornered, I know that a wise and
kind animal such as yourself would grant me one
last wish," Rabbit begged. "Please let me go home
to my family and say one last good-bye. You can
come to my house and get me. Just call me, and I
will leave my home forever."

Coyote was flattered. Not wanting to seem
heartless, he agreed to let Rabbit say one last good-
bye to his family. Besides, Rabbit would taste all
the sweeter a day later.

"You may go home now," Coyote said. "But be
prepared tomorrow morning to be my dinner."

Rabbit hopped home to his family. Hop! Hop!
Hop!

Coyote left for his cave home to prepare for a
feast.

Bright and early the next morning, Coyote
came running across the mesa toward Rabbit's
house. As he ran closer, he saw a strange line in the
distance. The unusual sight grew clearer to Coyote
as he neared Rabbit's home. To his surprise, Coyote
discovered all of Rabbit's friends and relations

standing shoulder to shoulder lined up across the desert. Coyote scratched his fur.

Which one was *his* rabbit? he wondered.

"Rabbit, I've come to get you," Coyote shouted uncertainly.

"Which rabbit are you speaking to?" the rabbits asked at the same time.

"The rabbit that walked by the cliff yesterday," Coyote answered.

"That's me." shouted all the rabbits. "I hopped by the cliff yesterday."

Coyote could see that he had been tricked once again. He sat down and yowled until he lost his voice. "OOhhhh. Ohhhh. Ohhh."

And the rabbits? They celebrated with a rabbit dance. Hop! Hop! Hop!

Share a Book

Coyotes and Rabbits

Aardema, Verna. *Borreguita and the Coyote.* Art by Petra Mathers. Random House, 1991. A little lamb tricks Coyote.

Bernard, Emery. *How Snowshoe Hare Rescued the Sun: A Tale from the Arctic.* Art by Durga Bernhard. Holiday House, 1993. Snowshoe Hare lives in the Arctic and rescues the sun from demons.

Goldin, Barbara Diamond. *Coyote and the Fire Stick.* Art by Will Hillenbrand. Gulliver/Harcourt, 1996. Coyote tries to get fire for the people.

Han, Suzanne Crowder. *The Rabbit's Judgment.* Art by Yumi Heo. Holt, 1994. Rabbit outwits Tiger to help a man in this story set in Korea.

Irbinskas, Heather. *How Jackrabbit Got His Very Long Ears.* Art by Kenneth J. Spengler. Northland, 1994. Jackrabbit learns to be kind to the other desert animals.

Johnston, Tony. *The Tale of Rabbit and Coyote.* Art by Tomie dePaola. Putnam, 1994. Rabbit tricks Coyote in a Zapotec tale.

Levy, Elizabeth. *Cleo and the Coyote.* Art by Diana Bryer. Harper, 1996. Cleo, a city dog, makes friends with a desert coyote.

Lund, Jillian. *Way Out West Lives a Coyote Named Frank.* Dutton, 1993. Two coyotes romp in the desert.

McDermott, Gerald. *Coyote.* Art by the author. Harcourt, 1994. In this Zuni tale, Coyote wants to learn to fly.

Pohrt, Tom. *Coyote Goes Walking.* Art by the author. Farrar, Strauss, 1995. Four short coyote adventures.

Stevens, Janet. *Coyote Steals the Blanket.* Art by the author. Holiday, 1993. In this Ute story, little Hummingbird warns Coyote not to be greedy and steal a blanket.

Stevens, Janet. *Old Bag of Bones.* Art by the author. Holiday, 1996. Coyote begs to be changed into a buffalo so he can be strong and powerful.

Taylor, Harriet Peck. *Coyote Places the Stars.* Art by the author. Bradbury, 1993. In this Wasco Indian legend, Coyote makes the constellations in the sky.

Taylor, Harriet Peck. *Coyote and the Laughing Butterflies.* Art by the author. Macmillan, 1995. Coyote is tricked by butterflies in this Tewa Indian legend.

Wood, Nancy. *The Girl Who Loved Coyotes: Stories of the Southwest.* Art by Diana Bryer. Morrow, 1995. Twelve original stories featuring Coyote and his tricks.

Friends

I don't know where the idea of friendship bracelets began, but I know they are popular with children. And adults like them too! Handwoven bracelets from Guatemala are one of my favorite presents to give.

Your group can weave bracelets for new or old friends, or they can decorate bracelets to promote their favorite books. Here are two different versions of friendship bracelets with book themes. These are faster and easier to make than Pedro's bracelets.

Craft a Paper Printed Bracelet

Supplies

duplicating machine

photocopy paper

paper cutter

art materials of your choice

clear tape

Preparation

Copy line-drawing designs (such as the one at the bottom of page 30) onto white paper. Cut the design strips apart.

Have children color the designs with art materials of your choice. Fasten the colored strips around each child's wrist with tape. If you are really in a hurry, duplicate the patterns on colored paper and give each child a bracelet to wear home.

Craft a Zigzag Paper Bracelet

Supplies

8-1/2" x 11" paper or precut 8" squares, preferably of
     paper colored on one side or wrapping paper

scissors

clear tape or glue

Preparation

If you use larger pages, fold the bottom edge beginning with the right-hand corner to align with the left edge of the paper. Cut off and discard the unfolded top section, leaving an 8" square. Cut along the fold, creating two triangles (1). These will make two bracelets, one for the crafter and one to give away. Now you are ready to put zigzag in the paper bracelet.

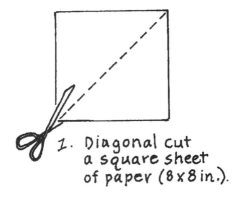

1. Diagonal cut a square sheet of paper (8 x 8 in.).

Place one triangle on a hard surface so it looks like a pyramid. Fold the bottom edge up about 5/8" (2). Continue this way, making accordion folds from the bottom until you have a small triangle flap left on top. Fold the triangle over the strip and tuck it into the first fold (3).

The tip of one end of the bracelet can thread into the other end to fit a wrist (4). Glue or tape the ends to hold them in shape.

If you used paper with one colored side, the bracelet will be more colorful. You automatically have a two-color ornament. The white surfaces that intertwine with the colored will accommodate a friend's name, the name of a favorite book, or a reading motto. If you don't have paper that is colored on only one side, let children make their own paper by drawing a repeated design on one side to create the same effect.

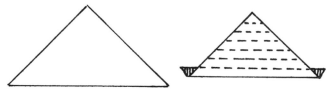

2. Accordion fold toward top of triangle.

3. Fold top of triangle over and tuck into fold.

4. Tuck one end into another to form bracelet.

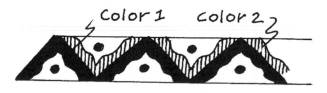

Color 1   Color 2

Create your own design.

Share a Story

Pedro's Idea

Caroline Feller Bauer

Pedro's grandmother wove fabric on a wooden loom. His mother fashioned the weaving into shirts for men and skirts for women. Pedro's job was to carry the goods to the market in Chichicastenango twice a week.

Years ago only local Mayan Indians and a few travelers from Guatemala City attended the market. Now tourists from many different countries filled the market. There were families touring from neighboring Latin American countries. There were students from the universities in

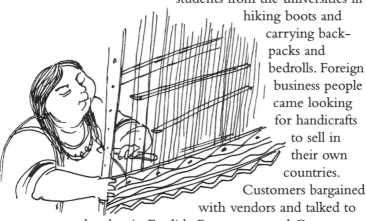

hiking boots and carrying back-packs and bedrolls. Foreign business people came looking for handicrafts to sell in their own countries. Customers bargained with vendors and talked to each other in English, Portuguese, and German, languages far beyond Pedro's Mayan language and limited Spanish.

Pedro longed to sell something that he had made himself. Guatemalan men sometimes carved and painted masks to sell, but weaving was usually considered women's work. Still, weaving threads and yarn into cloth fascinated Pedro. He could watch his mother and grandmother weave for hours. He wanted to weave, too. Only his idea was to make placemats and napkins for the tourists.

At first, his mother scoffed at the idea. Who ever heard of putting their beautiful weaving on the table and covering it with a dish? The idea seemed ridiculous. After much pleading from Pedro, his mother made a few placemats—just to try. To her surprise, the placemats sold.

Then Pedro had another idea. This time, he would weave something simple and fast. He knew how his grandmother wove the wool. He was sure he could weave beautiful patterns, too. So he built a small loom with several sticks and took some wool from the discard basket. He quickly wove a thin strip of multicolored wool with string ends dangling on each side.

Pedro inspected his work. He smiled. Only a few bumps poked from the fabric.

Pedro's sister, Maria, was amused. "What's that?" she asked giggling.

"I'm not sure," Pedro answered. "Maybe it could mark the place in a book when a person stops reading."

"Yes, perhaps," she agreed. "I've seen Señor Marquez place a bit of paper to mark his account book."

Pedro wove a few more bookmarks. With each strip he finished, Pedro made fewer mistakes.

On market day, Pedro and Maria carried the usual bundle of shirts and skirts down the mountain to the market. Pedro hid a handful of the new bookmarks in his pocket. Throughout the morning, all Maria and Pedro sold were two shirts to a large man who swung his arms wildly as he bargained.

Then Pedro saw a bus filled with tourists arrive in the market square. He left Maria in charge of the booth, removed the bookmarks from his pocket, and ran to the door of the bus, waving the cloth strips. Pedro hoped a scholar who read books would buy them. Alas, hardly anyone glanced at his colorful bands.

Then Pedro followed a group of the tourists while they visited each stall. As they turned to another stall, Pedro held up the bookmarks with pleading eyes. Some seemed cranky and waved him away, but Pedro doggedly followed them. They didn't understand his language. He didn't understand theirs.

Suddenly, someone tapped him on the shoulder. It was the same man with the wild arms who had bought the shirts earlier. "I'd like one of those," he said in Spanish. "In fact, I'd like 100 of them for a good price."

"I don't have a 100," Pedro said in halting Spanish. "But I can get them by tomorrow."

"Excellent," said the man. "Please deliver them to the White Hotel tomorrow by 9:00 A.M. Ask for Señor Lopez."

Pedro was ecstatic. Señor Lopez must read a lot!

When he returned to the stall, Pedro told Maria about his bookmarks and the large man. "We must go home at once," he said. "Somehow I must weave another eighty bookmarks by morning."

The two packed up and raced to their village. Their mother was pleased that they had sold two shirts.

"But why have you returned so early?" his grandmother asked. Pedro told the women about the bookmarks he made and the gigantic order for 100.

"We will all help weave the strips," his grand-mother said.

Now Pedro was the teacher. He showed his whole family how to fashion a simple loom and weave the strips. "I guess the señor doesn't care what color they are," Pedro said. "Let's use whatever wool we have in the discard basket."

The family worked together until sundown. They woke at the first hint of light the next morning to finish the strips. Tired but triumphant, Pedro and Maria walked down the mountain to the White Hotel at the entrance of the now vacant market.

Neither Maria nor Pedro had ever entered the hotel before. Their eyes darted from side to side taking in the sights. The hotel was beautiful. Guests ate breakfast at small tables in front of a fountain. Many wore little signs on their clothes with names.

Señor Lopez saw Pedro and called for him and Maria to come to his table. Señor Lopez briefly examined the bookmarks and gave Pedro a handful of money. "And here is a little something extra for the fast work," Señor Lopez added. "What is your name?"

"Stand here," Señor Lopez said after Pedro told him. "You will see who receives your fine work." Señor Lopez stood up, took a spoon, and hit his coffee cup. Everyone quieted.

"Ladies and gentlemen. We have come together for this meeting in friendship and common under-standing. In only a few days we have accomplished a lot. I feel confident that each of us will return to our countries with a sense of hope and renewal. As the delegate from the host country of Guatemala, I would like to give each of you a token of our friendship. This young crafter has made each of you a circle of friendship, a bracelet of friendship to remember our time together."

The people at the tables with the little name tags on their clothes applauded. Although he understood little of what Señor Lopez said, Pedro knew the applause was for him. Pedro stood proudly and smiled.

Then Señor Lopez asked Pedro and Maria to help pass out the bracelets.

As they came to one of the tables, a woman spoke in Spanish with an American accent. "These are lovely," she said. "Do you have any extras? My granddaughter is having a birthday party. I know she would like to give each of her friends one of your friendship bracelets."

Pedro turned to Maria and spoke in Mayan. "These are no longer bookmarks. They are friendship bracelets."

He turned to the woman and asked, "How many friends does your granddaughter have? And how soon do you need them?"

Share a Book

Friends

Gryski, Camilla. *Friendship Bracelets.* Art by Pixel Graphics. Morrow, 1993. Step-by-step instructions for creating embroidery thread friendship bracelets.

Henkes, Kevin. *A Weekend with Wendell.* Art by the author. Greenwillow, 1986. Sophie learns to get along with Wendell in a mouse story of learning to be a good friend.

Hilton, Nette. *Andrew Jessup.* Art by Cathy Wilcox. Ticknor, 1992. Andrew moved out of town, and the new neighbor is a new friend but different from Andrew.

James, Simon. *Leon and Bob.* Art by the author. Candlewick, 1997. Bob is Leon's imaginary friend, but then he meets a new friend whose name is Bob.

Kasza, Keiko. *The Rat and the Tiger.* Art by the author. Putnam, 1993. Rat is the boss until Rat teaches Tiger to share.

Katz, Bobbi. *Could We Be Friends?* Poems for Pals. Art by Joung Un Kim. Mondo, 1997. Picture book collection of friendship poems.

Mavor, Salley, ed. *You and Me: Poems of Friendship.* Art by the editor. Orchard, 1997. A picture book collection of poems featuring the topic friendship and illustrated with soft sculpture.

Pryor, Bonnie. *Louie and Dan Are Friends.* Art by Elizabeth Miles. Morrow, 1997. Two mouse brothers are best friends but have very different temperaments.

Raschka, Chris. *Yo! Yes!* Art by the author. Orchard, 1993. Two boys meet and begin a new friendship.

Reiser, Lynn. *Margaret and Margarita.* Art by the author. Greenwillow, 1993. Margaret speaks English. Margarita speaks Spanish. They meet in the park and play learning words from each other's language.

Seabrook, Elizabeth. *Cabbages and Kings.* Art by Jamie Wyeth. Viking, 1997. An asparagus stalk makes friends with a cabbage.

Uchida, Yoshiko. *The Bracelet.* Art by Joanna Yardley. Philomel, 1993. In this World War II Japanese internment story, Emi loses the bracelet given to her by her best friend but learns that the friendship is forever.

Hats

When I was growing up, a man or a woman was considered improperly dressed if they were not wearing a hat. Today, one rarely sees a fashionable hat, unless you consider baseball caps a fashion statement. Yet, hats are fun—for special events, for dressing up, for acting out many different fun stories about hats!

Craft a Hat

Supplies

ruler

poster paper (construction paper works, although not as
     well, but is less expensive)

scissors

art materials of your choice

decorations of your choice, for example, sequins, feath-
     ers, beads, buttons, glitter, yarn, tissue paper scraps,
     torn paper pieces

glue

stapler (optional)

Preparation

Measure strips of poster paper that are about 1-1/2" x 28" and cut one for each child. Shorten the length if the hats are for smaller children.

Cut one end of the strip with a hook shape to serve as a fastener. Score several slits halfway into the strip along the top edge of the other end. Measure the slits about 1/2" apart (1).

Cut enough hat patterns for children to either trace their own pattern or keep to decorate for their own hat (2). Cut two parallel slits in the center of each hat pattern to thread the hooked strip through (3).

cut slits

Depending upon your group, you may want children to measure and cut their own strips and hat shapes of their own design. Give children a choice of materials and art supplies to decorate their hats. Emphasize that there is probably a story or poem to go with every style hat. If not, they can surely make one up. Reinforce this information by sharing the following examples.

Share a Story

Everybody has a birthday, and everybody loves a birthday party. Maybe that's why books about birthdays are so popular. Tell children about this special birthday book that includes hats, cowboy hats.

In *Harry's Birthday* by Barbara Ann Porte, Harry plans his birthday party. He wants a gala event with ice cream and cake, balloons and streamers, games and prizes. And, of course, he wants presents.

Harry tells everyone what he wants. "I'm hoping for a cowboy hat," he tells his father, relatives, and friends. Does he get what he wants? Let's let Harry tell you what happened at his party.

Harry's Birthday

Barbara Ann Porte

"Make a wish," my father says.

I close my eyes. *Please let one of my presents be a cowboy hat.*

Then I blow out all of the candles in one breath. Everyone claps.

I slice the first slice, then Pop cuts the rest.

Aunt Rose and Uncle Leo scoop ice cream, pour fruit punch, help serve.

Afterward we play games. Dorcas wins pin the tail on the donkey.

"I think she could see," Edith whispers.

"I could not, either," says Dorcas.

Uncle Leo plays the tuba for musical chairs. Barry wins.

"I would have won, except he tripped me," says Edna.

"Time to open the presents," my father says, carrying them in. I sit on the floor, with everyone else in a circle around me.

"Open mine first," say some of the guests.

"Don't open mine first," say the rest.

Pop hands me a present from the top.

"That's mine," says Eddie.

I take off the paper and open the box. Inside is a red cowboy hat with a black band all around it and cords that hang down to tie under my chin. I try it on. It fits perfectly.

"Thank you," I say. "It's just what I wanted."

"I know," says Eddie.

I open my next present.

"That's mine," says José.

I take out a black cowboy hat with a red band all around it and cords that hang down to tie under my chin. I try it on. It fits perfectly, too.

"Thank you," I say. "It's just what I wanted."

"I know," says José.

My next present is from Edith. It is a white cowboy hat with a matching band and cords that hang down to tie under my chin.

"Thank you," I say. "It's just what I wanted." I try hard to sound sincere.

"I thought so," says Edith.

By the time I have opened all my presents, I have seven cowboy hats, including a ten-gallon one from my father.

I also have a pair of cowboy boots from Aunt Rose and Uncle Leo, a book on juggling from Dorcas, a baseball cap and bat from Barry and Edna, and a dozen gingerbread people.

"My mom forgot to buy something, so she baked instead," says Martin. "I hope you like them."

"Oh, I do," I tell him. . . .

(Tell children that you are skipping some of the story about the rest of what happens at the party. Then continue with the closing.)

After all the guests have left and we have straightened the house, Uncle Leo says, "What interesting presents. Harry could open a hat store."

"Sure he could," Aunt Rose says, smiling. "But if I had so many nice hats, I'd hang them all on the wall for decoration. Well, except for the one I was wearing."

"What a good idea!" my father says.

I think so, too.

So that's what we do. Pop gets a hammer, nails, hooks, and a tape measure from the basement. Uncle Leo measures the wall and pencils X's in all the right places. Aunt Rose holds up the hooks and bangs in the nails.

Then I stand on my step stool and hang all my hats in a circle, except for the one I am wearing. "I think they look very nice hanging there," I say.

"Sure they do," says Uncle Leo. . . .

"Happy birthday, Harry."

Share a Story

Each child can create a fez and wear it at the end of the story. To get in the mood for fez hats yourself, read the adult book *A Fez in the Heart: Travel around Turkey in Search of a Hat* by Jeremy Seal for fun. Here is a story for children.

The Fez

Retold by

Caroline Feller Bauer

In the olden days, Je, the Sultan of Fez, was very pleased with almost everything in his life. Je loved his palace. He loved his town. He appreciated the fact that there was enough water in his desert town to support a large population.

He was unhappy about only one thing. Few people had heard of the city of Fez. He wanted to put Fez on the world map. So Je sent out a proclamation. Whoever could think of an idea for putting Fez on the world map would be given a bag of gold.

Naturally, many people tried for the bag of gold. One man said: "I'm sure that you have heard of Jerusalem. The King there has many wives. If you had many wives I'm sure that everyone would soon hear of Fez. I have a pretty daughter. She could be one of your wives."

"No, thank you," the Sultan said. "I don't think my wife would like that idea."

Another man talked about the senate in Rome. "If you had a similar body of government here in Fez, everyone would know about Fez. I could be one of your senators."

"No, thank you," the Sultan said. "I like ruling by myself."

Many more townspeople offered their ideas. The
sultan rejected them all. Then a young man from
the mountains presented himself to the
sultan.

"I have an idea for putting Fez on the map," he
said. "Here it is, Your Majesty." The man held up
something in his hand.

"What's that?" the sultan
asked.

"It's a hat, Your Majesty,"
the young man
answered. "Put it on. It
blocks the sun from
your head and keeps the
flies away."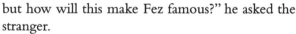

The sultan tried on
the hat. Indeed, it did
block the sun from his
head and keep the
flies away. "I like it,
but how will this make Fez famous?" he asked the
stranger.

"Well, your honor, the hat is called a fez," the
man answered. "If you wear one, everyone in town
will want one. If everyone in town is wearing one,
travelers will want one to take back to their
homes. Soon, everyone in the world will be wearing a fez. Everyone will know where the hat came
from—the city of Fez."

"Great idea," the sultan said. "Here is your bag
of gold."

"Oh, no, thank you," the young man said. "I
don't need the gold."

"What do you mean, you don't need gold?" the
sultan wondered. "Everyone wants to be rich."

"I will be rich," the young man said. "I'm going
to sell everyone his fez."

Share a Poem

The most fun often comes from making up poems, especially ones that include something about the children. After crafters decorate their hats, have a hat parade to show them off. Accompany the parade with a hat parade chant.

Big hats
Small hats
Red hats
Blue hats
Plain hats
High hats
We love hats.

(Now add names of children in the group.)

Harry's hat
Hilary's hat
Peter's hat
We love hats.

Abul's hat
Annie's hat
Paul's hat
Karen's hat
We love hats.

Share a Book

Hats

Bancroft, Catherine, and Hannah Coale Gruenberg. *Felix's Hat*. Art by Hannah Coale Gruenberg. Four Winds, 1993.

Felix's head doesn't feel happy without his favorite cap.

Brett, Jan. *The Hat*. Art by the author. Putnam, 1997. The other animals make fun of a hedgehog wearing clothes, but they end up wearing clothes, too.

Clark, Emma Chichester. *Catch That Hat!* Art by the author. Little, Brown, 1990. Rose and her animal friends chase a hat blown by the wind around the countryside.

Gardella, Tricia. *Casey's New Hat*. Art by Margot Apple. Houghton, 1997. Casey tries a number of hats, but Grandpa's old hat has the perfect fit.

Howard, Elizabeth. *Aunt Flossie's Hats (and Crab Cakes Later)*. Art by James Ransome. Clarion, 1991. Great-aunt Flossie tells a story for each one of the hats in the boxes and boxes and boxes of hats.

Kroll, Steven. *Princess Abigail and the Wonderful Hat*. Art by Patience Brewster. Holiday, 1991. Although Prince Grindstone wins the design for the best hat, the Princess refuses to marry him.

Lattimore, Deborah Nourse. *The Lady with the Ship on Her Head*. Art by the author. Harcourt, 1990. While competing for the best headdress, Madame Pompenstance is unaware that a ship has sailed onto her head.

Lowell, Susan. *Little Red Cowboy Hat*. Art by Randy Cecil. Holt, 1997. This variant of the Little Red Riding Hood story is set in the West with a spunky Grandma.

Milich, Melissa. *Miz Fannie Mae's Fine New Easter Hat*. Art by Yong Chen. Little, Brown, 1997. The eggs on Mama's beautiful new Easter hat hatch in church.

Morris, Ann. *Hats Hats Hats.* Photos by Ken Heyman. Lothrop, 1989. Photo essay shows people wearing a variety of hats around the world.

Pearson, Tracey Campbell. *The Purple Hat.* Art by the author. Farrar, 1997. Annie's purple hat is lost on a field trip. Where can it be?

Schneider, Howie. *Uncle Lester's Hat.* Art by the author. Putnam, 1997. Uncle Wilford chases his hat around the world. Funny!

Smath, Jerry. *A Hat So Simple.* Art by the author. BridgeWater, 1993. Edna decorates her hat but decides that a simpler hat is better for fishing.

Stoeke, Janet Morgan. *A Hat for Minerva Louise.* Art by the author. Dutton, 1994. Minerva the chicken finally finds the perfect hat to keep her warm—actually, she finds two hats and a pair of mittens.

Houses

Houses vary with cultures, but the most important aspect of a house is that it represents *home* to each of us. Challenge children to imagine as many different kinds of homes as they can. Remind them that various homes have been the subject of countless books and poems, beginning with cave homes and later mud homes, huts, log cabins, and castles. Explain that some of the stories you will read connect with these houses.

Craft a Peek-A-Boo House

Supplies

two sheets of construction paper

scissors

glue

art materials of your choice

Preparation

Draw an outline of a house or apartment building on one of the papers to reproduce, or ask each child to draw their own. Make sure the house fills the page, so it is large enough for at least four sizable windows and a door. Cut into three sides of each window and the door. The fourth side should fold back to form a flap (1).

Glue the house onto the second sheet of paper. Be careful not to glue where the window and door flaps are.

Discuss with the children what the interiors of the homes and apartments might look like and who might live in them. Tell them to think of a story about these imaginary characters and their homes. Perhaps the people who live there are planning for a visit from a favorite aunt, or maybe the children inside the home are on school vacation or chasing their mischievous dog.

Have the children draw these people, animals, and activities inside the flaps of their paper home. Suggest that behind each flap they could either draw a different stage

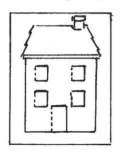

of the same storyline, a different activity from the story, or the varied members of the household. Encourage children to add details of what they think each room should look like, such as wallpaper, wall hangings, furniture, and favorite possessions (2).

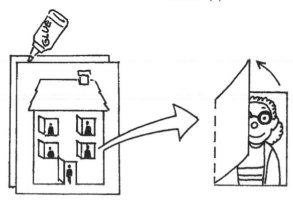

If time permits and your group has the skills, you can extend this and the other craft house activity. After completing the peek-a-boo house, ask the children to write a story about the subjects—people or animals—who live in the house. When they finish writing the story, glue a copy to the back of the house. Have boys and girls share their story with the group, showing the house as a visual for the story.

Craft a
Paper Dream House

Supplies

one sheet of 11" x 17" legal paper

1/4 sheet of 8-1/2" x 11" paper

clear tape or glue

art materials of your choice to decorate the house

Preparation

You might want to experiment with patterns before presenting the activity. These houses/buildings can be made in all sizes. Prepare enough patterns for your group.

Have children cut the house and roof from the patterns (1). Direct kids to fold along the dotted lines. Then they can glue or tape the walls of the house together, and add the roof (2). Suggest that they decorate with a variety of art supplies, everything from coloring materials to gluing textured items, such as cheerios, rice, or candies (3). Decorations may be easier to add before the house is taped together. Children may want to create a town or table display to accompany an exhibit of books about houses.

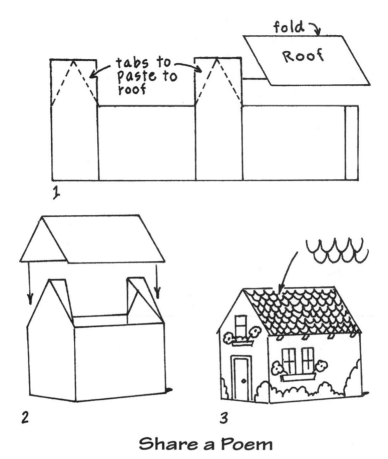

Share a Poem

Read the first verse of this poem aloud without giving the title. Ask children to draw a picture that goes with what they heard. What type of room was described in the poem? What features, if any, did it have?

Now read the whole poem to the group. Show them how the poet designed the poem on the page. Mention how you had to read the poem from the top down in the first column and then from the bottom up in the second column in order for the poem to make sense. Discuss whether their drawings look like the elevator described in this poem.

Elevator

Sylvia Cassedy

DOWN	One wall	more
	a door,	or
	the	away
	others	feet
	bare;	ty
	no	nine-
	win-	later
	dow,	ment
	table,	mo-
	pic-	a
	ture,	just
	chair;	exit
	a gloom-	and
	y,	door
	tomb-	gle
	like	sin-
	room,	its
	and	through
	small—	Enter
	no	vator.
	larger	ele-
	than	the
	a	room
	show-	a
	er	odd
	stall.	How UP

After reading the poem, have children complete the *Tell and Draw a House* activity. To begin this activity, ask kids to imagine a home. Tell them that it could be their home, a pretend home in this or another time, or a home for an animal or other creature. It could be a house, apartment, castle, cottage, or home from outer space.

Direct the girls and boys to write a description of this home. Once they are finished, have the children choose partners and exchange their descriptions. Pass out paper and art materials of your choice. Then ask the kids to draw the house that is detailed in their partner's description.

If children are too young or the group too unwieldy for each person to write their own descriptions, the leader can give the entire group an oral description of a home to draw. Allow time for children to display their pictures and describe their homes together.

Share a Book

Houses

Calhoun, Mary. *Flood*. Art by Erick Ingraham. Morrow, 1997. Forced to leave their home in the Midwest floods of 1993, Sarajean learns that home is where the family is.

Howard, Ellen. *The Log Cabin Quilt*. Art by Ronald Himler. Holiday House, 1996. Grandma's quilting scraps help keep the cold from penetrating a log cabin.

Neitzel, Shirley. *The House I'll Build for the Wrens*. Art by Nancy Winslow Parker. Greenwillow, 1997. A little boy borrows tools from his mother to build a house for birds in this cumulative rhythmic picture book.

Platt, Richard. *The Apartment Book: A Day in Five Stories*. Art by Leo Hartas. Dorling Kindersley, 1995. Oversized detailed art highlights the activities of people living and visiting in a five-story apartment building.

Ray, Jane. *Hansel and Gretel*. Art by the author. Candlewick Press, 1997. A modern rendition of the traditional story of two lost children enticed by a candy house owned by a wicked witch.

Rounds, Glen. *Sod Houses on the Great Plains.* Art by the author. Holiday House, 1995. In a light-hearted romp, Rounds shows how a "soddie" was built.

Ventura, Piero. *Houses.* Art by the author. Houghton Mifflin, 1992. A history of home building from caves to the modern apartment.

Wilder, Laura Ingalls. *Little House on the Prairie.* Original art by Helen Sewell. Harper & Brothers, 1935. Classic series set during pioneer days.

Williams, Brian. *Forts and Castles.* Art by the author. Viking, 1994. See-through overlays help the reader understand the building of castles and forts.

Mr. Riddle and
Dr. Twist

se these finger puppets to dance and play to riddles and tongue twisters.

Craft Finger Dancing Puppets

Supplies

at least one 3" x 5" index card for each person

scissors

art materials of your choice

Preparation

Copy or trace outlines of these figures onto index cards, and cut the sample shapes. Show the children how to fold a bottom flap back at least 1-1/4" at the base of the card (1). Tell them to outline the figure they choose onto their index card above the fold. You can also encourage children to create their own people/animals/objects.

Then have everyone decorate their figures, adding facial details, clothes, and so on. Direct them to cut two holes in the folded flap (2) for the puppeteers to insert their fingers to make the puppets dance (3).

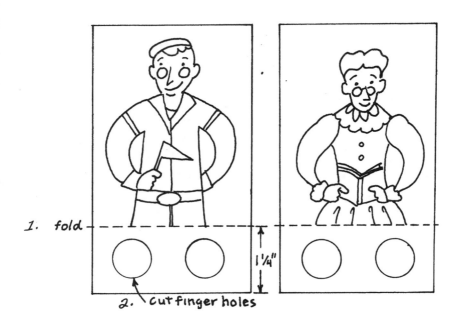

1. **fold**

1¼"

2. cut finger holes

3.

Share Tongue Twisters

Tell children to let the puppets repeat these tongue twisters several times while dancing on their fingers. You may want children to form groups for this activity. Or you could invite a few children to say the tongue twisters together while hiding their bodies behind a table in front of the larger group. The table becomes the impromptu puppet stage with only the puppet showing.

Here are some tongue twisters to repeat:

- truly rural
- mixed biscuits
- lemon liniment
- Sally sells seashells by the seashore.
- Ruth's red roof
- Ramrod Roy rakes rain.

Share Riddles

Choose two different children for each riddle. Have one puppet ask the other:

JAKE: My cat can talk.

MARTA: Really?

JAKE: Yes. I asked her, "What's four minus four and she said nothing."

JAKE: Mom, remember how you were always worried that I'd break your heirloom vase?

MOM: Yes?

JAKE: Well, your worries are over.

MARTA: I'm calling to make an appointment with the dentist.

JAKE: Sorry. The dentist isn't in the office today.

MARTA: Good. When will he be out of the office again?

MARTA: My dog is a baseball dog.

JAKE: What's a baseball dog?

MARTA: A dog that wears a muzzle, catches flies, chases fouls, and runs for home when she sees the catcher coming.

MARTA: What's the difference between a carton of milk and a giraffe?

JAKE: I don't know.

MARTA: Well, if you don't know the difference, I certainly won't send you to the store for a carton of milk.

Share a Book

Funny Stories

Clement, Rod. *Just Another Ordinary Day.* Art by the author. Harpercollins, 1997. The day in the book may sound ordinary, but if you share the pictures you will see that Amanda lives in an amazing world with dinosaurs, giant bug teachers, and junk food in the school cafeteria.

Compton, Joanne. *Sody Sallyratus.* Art by Ken Compton. Holiday House, 1995. In this version of the popular folktale, Jack tries to find out what happened to Ma and his two brothers on the way to the store.

Enderle, Judith Ross, and Stephanie Gordon Tessler. *Where Are You, Little Zack?* Art by Brian Floca. Houghton Mifflin, 1997. A duck family and lots of people search for little Zack Quack.

Faulkner, Keith. *The Wide-Mouthed Frog.* Art by Jonathan Lambert. Dial, 1996. The wide-mouthed frog learns not to be quite so inquisitive in this pop-up version of the tale.

Jorensen, Gail. *Gotcha!* Art by Kerry Argent. Scholastic, 1995. A bear chases a pesky fly with laugh-aloud results.

Nikola-Lisa, W. *Tangle Talk.* Art by Jessica Clerk. Dutton, 1997. Upside-down events in the "month of Boston, in the wonderful city of May."

Riddles

Share riddles from these books between storybooks and activities. Riddles serve as attention-getters and funny bone ticklers. There seems to be a riddle for every subject.

Hall, Katy. *Puppy Riddles.* Art by Thor Wickstrom. Dial, 1998.

Joyce, Susan. *Alphabet Riddles.* Art by Doug DuBosque. Peel, 1998.

Phillips, Louis. *Monster Riddles.* Art by Arlene Dubanevich. Viking, 1998.

Seltzer, Meyer. *Petcetera: The Pet Riddle Book.* Albert Whitman, 1988.

Names

I spent a lot of time as a youngster playing with my name, writing it in block letters and script and cutting it out in construction paper. The C in Caroline was always hard to get right. Our daughter's name is Hilary, and I think *H* is much easier to cut from paper.

Do you have a story about your name—perhaps how you got your name or nickname—that you could share with your group? A story is a great way to introduce the topic of names as a theme for books, plays, and poems. Moreover, a craft is a fun avenue for expressing something that is so personal for us all—our name.

Craft a Name Necklace

Supplies

an index card for each person

yarn or string (about 2-1/2' for each person)

single hole punch

art supplies of your choice

Preparation

Give each person an index card and coloring materials. Ask them to write their name to fill the card. Then have them decorate their name in some way. They could draw the letters in different colors, make block letters to fill in the outline with designs, write jumping letters rather than in a straight line.

When the cards are decorated, punch two holes along the top edge of the card. Thread a piece of yarn through the holes, and tie the ends together to form a necklace.

Group the children to exchange stories about their names. If individuals complain they don't have a story, tell them to make up one about their name or someone else's. Some suggestions include:

- How did you get your name?
- Do you have a nickname? If so, how did you get this name?
- What name would you choose if you could have any name? Why?
- Do you have a story about one of your friends' or relatives' names?
- What are your favorite names? Are there reasons for your choices?

Share a Poem

This is a good silly poem to read aloud, to have children take turns reading, or for you to summarize.

Too Many Daves

Dr. Seuss

Did I ever tell you that Mrs. McCave
Had twenty-three sons and she named them all Dave?
Well, she did. And that wasn't a smart thing to do.
You see, when she wants one and calls out, "Yoo-Hoo!
Come into the house, Dave!" she doesn't get *one*.
All twenty-three Daves of hers come on the run!
This makes things quite difficult at the McCaves'
As you can imagine, with so many Daves.
And often she wishes that, when they were born,
She had named one of them Bodkin Van Horn
And one of them Hoos-Foos. And one of them Snimm.
And one of them Hot-Shot. And one Sunny Jim.
And one of them Shadrack. And one of them Blinkey.
And one of them Stuffy. And one of them Stinkey.
Another one Putt-Putt. Another one Moon Face.
Another one Marvin O'Gravel Balloon Face.
And one of them Ziggy. And one Soggy Muff.
One Buffalo Bill. And one Biffalo Buff.
And one of them Sneepy. And one Weepy Weed.
And one Paris Garters. And one Harris Tweed.
And one of them Sir Michael Carmichael Zutt
And one of them Oliver Boliver Butt
And one of them Zanzibar Buck-Buck McFate . . .
But she didn't do it. And now it's too late.

Craft Stick Puppets

Supplies

poster board or other stiff paper

crayons

scissors

glue, rubber cement, or clear tape

popsicle sticks or tongue depressors (available at craft or
drug stores)

Preparation

Copy the pictures from pages 63-69 on poster board, and
cut enough patterns for your group. Tell children they are
going to put on a puppet show about names. The show is
based on the story Yung-Kyung-Pyung, a Jamaican tale of
Anansi the Spider Man. Before they present the play, children will make the characters.

Show the different characters and objects from the
play, and ask kids to choose one to color. After children
decorate their puppet, help them attach each puppet to a
stick with tape or glue. Make sure the colored side faces
outward and enough of the stick appears from the bottom
of the picture for a child to grasp.

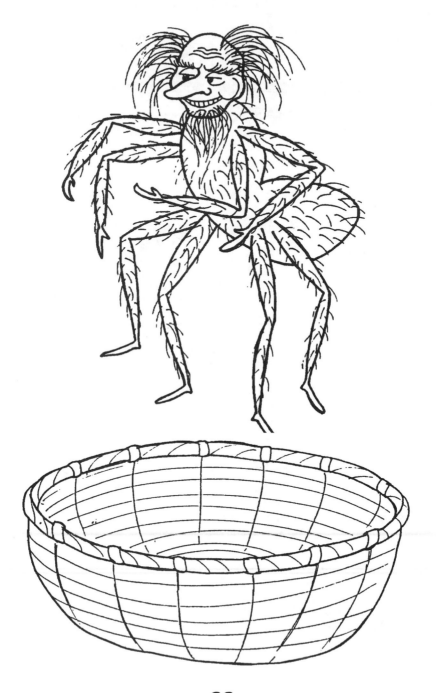

Share a Play

Use the play as a reader's theater piece. Parts can be assigned and read aloud. If you are selecting different characters, prepare enough copies of the play for each puppeteer. A wide table can function as a puppet stage, if you do not have one. Players can crouch behind the table, or simply hold the puppets while they act out the story.

Yung-Kyung-Pyung
Anansi, the Spider Man: Jamaican Folk Tales
Adapted by Philip M. Sherlock

CHARACTERS:

King, Anansi, Crow, Rat, Bullfrog, Eggie-Law, Yung-Kyung-Pyung, Marg'ret-Powell-Alone, Narrator

NARRATOR: A King had three daughters. No one in the kingdom knew their names. Many had tried to guess their names, but all failed. Anansi thought he would try his luck.

ANANSI: I'm going to fill a basket with fruit. I'm going to fill it with mangoes, bananas, oranges, and paw-paw. Now I will leave it by the side of the river where the King's daughters are swimming.

NARRATOR: Anansi hid behind a tree, listened, and watched.

EGGIE-LAW: Yung-Kyung-Pyung! What a pretty basket! Marg'ret-Powell-Alone! What a pretty basket!

YUNG-KYUNG-PYUNG: Marg'ret-Powell-Alone! What a pretty basket! Eggie-Law! What a pretty basket!

MARG'RET-POWELL-ALONE: Eggie-Law! What a pretty basket! Yung-Kyung-Pung! What a pretty basket!

EGGIE, YUNG, MARG'RET: Let's go and show the basket to our father, the King.

NARRATOR: Anansi heard and saw the girls. He went back to his home town and gathered together a little band of musicians.

ANANSI: Rat, Crow, Bullfrog. Help me earn some money. I need you to play a tune in front of the King's castle.

RAT: I will play.

CROW: I will play.

BULLFROG: I will play.

NARRATOR: The little band of musicians practiced all week. On Saturday, Anansi, Crow, Bullfrog, and Rat stood in front of the King's castle.

RAT, CROW, BULLFROG SINGING TOGETHER AND PLAYING MUSIC:

Yung-Kyung-Pyung, Eggie-Law, Marg'ret-Powell-Alone! Yung-Kyung-Pyung, Eggie-Law, Marg'ret-Powell-Alone! Yung-Kyung-Pyung, Eggie-Law, Marg'ret-Powell-Alone!

KING: Who is calling the names of my daughters?

ANANSI: It is Anansi.

BULLFROG: It is Bullfrog.

CROW: It is Crow.

RAT: It is Rat.

KING: Come in. You may have anything you wish from the castle.

BULLFROG: I would like a bag of silver.

CROW: I would like a bag of gold.

ANANSI: I would like a bag of gold and silver.

NARRATOR: Rat was the cleverest of all. He chose to marry the King's eldest daughter Yung-Kyung-Pyung.

RAT AND YUNG: And we lived happily ever after.

ALL: The End

Share a Story

Candy
Caroline Feller Bauer

It was the first day of school. A new teacher stood in the front of the fourth grade classroom.

"Welcome to my first day and your first day of school," she said. "My name is Ms. Katherine Wilkins, and I'd like you to introduce yourselves to me. Please give me your first and last name. If you have a nickname, I'd like to know that, too."

There were several children in the class who had not attended Abigail Adams School last year. MaryAnn was new, just like the teacher. MaryAnn, however, didn't like her name very much. Yet, when it was her turn, she managed to speak up loudly and clearly, "My name is MaryAnn Potatoes."

No one laughed. That was a good sign to MaryAnn. She refused to tell the class that in her old school her nickname was French Fry.

Still, she thought it was fun to have a nickname. Last week she had spent the night at her grandparent's house. They had watched an old movie about a determined girl and her horse, *National Velvet*.

"From now on, my nickname will be Velvet," MaryAnn had said firmly. Maybe her new classmates could call her Velvet. In fact, maybe she could win a horse like the girl in the movie.

MaryAnn listened with interest as the other students gave their names. One girl at the next table caught her eye. She had an interesting hairdo. Her hair was long on one side and short on the other.

When it was the girl's turn to give her name, MaryAnn discovered that the girl also had an interesting name. "My name is CANDY Cotton," she said. MaryAnn thought the girl must surely be called "Cotton Candy" by everyone.

Ms. Wilkins asked if that was her real name or her nickname. "My name is CANDY, but it's just a bunch of initials. It's C-A-N-D-Y. The C is for Caroline."

"Your real name is Caroline Cotton?" Ms. Wilkins asked.

"No, no," Candy said. "Caroline is just part of the name. Then comes A for Alice."

"Caroline Alice," Ms. Wilkins repeated. "How pretty."

"That's not my whole name either," CANDY said. "Then comes N for Nanette."

"Your name is Caroline Alice Nanette?" Ms. Wilkins asked, wondering how many more names Candy could have.

"Not exactly. Then comes D for Dorothy," Candy said.

"Now, I understand," said Ms. Wilkins. "Your name is Caroline, Alice, Nanette, Dorothy, and I guess there is still another name for the letter Y."

"You guessed it," Candy said. "My name stands for Caroline Alice Nanette Dorothy Yvonne, but my real name is C-A-N-D-Y."

"An impressive name. How did you get such an interesting long name?" Ms. Wilkins asked.

Candy tried to explain. "My Mom and Dad both have sisters. They wanted to name me after one of the sisters, but which one to choose? So, I have all their names: Aunt Caroline, Aunt Alice, Aunt Nanette, Aunt Dorothy, and Aunt Yvonne. It's easy to remember my aunts' names. They are my name: C-A-N-D-Y."

"Your name is awesome," MaryAnn said.

"Are you named for Velvet in the film *National Velvet?*" Candy asked.

"How did you guess?" answered MaryAnn, now Velvet.

From then on, MaryAnn knew she had found a new friend. This person had seen and loved the same film as she had, and her name was C-A-N-D-Y.

After telling this story, you may want to play some name games. Here are a few suggestions. Plan ahead for the games by having enough paper and pencils or crayons available.

NAME SCRAMBLE

Before the children arrive, divide their names into groups. Scramble the name of each member in each group on a piece of paper, for example, *eraoilnc* for Caroline. Copy enough scrambled name lists for each person on the list. Tell participants to see who in each group can unscramble the names on their list first.

NAME BOOK TITLES

Instruct boys and girls to make up a story title that uses each letter of their name. For example, the name *Hilary* could be the title "How Inconsiderate, Larry Ate Ron's Yo-Yo." Encourage creativity, even silliness. Then ask the children to write a story that goes with their title. Allow time to share the stories.

BIG WORDS FROM LITTLE WORDS

This is one of my favorite activities. Select helpers to pass out a sheet of paper and a pencil to each child. Tell girls and boys to write their full name on top of the page. Then ask them to write as many words as they can using only the letters in their name.

NAME REMEMBERING GAME

Do you ever have trouble remembering the names of people you have just met? I do. Here is a way to help children recall names of others. Have them practice by pairing with a partner and introducing themselves. Tell children to repeat the name back to the person for reinforcement.

Then they are to associate their partner's name with a picture in their head. For example, my name is Caroline. If you were my partner, you might imagine a car swinging on a line or someone singing Christmas carols. The important thing is you see action in your picture.

When everyone imagines a picture, ask them to draw the picture that represents the name of their partner. If you prefer, the children can use their own names instead. Either way, display the pictures and have everyone guess whose name is represented.

Share a Book

Names

There are two traditional stories that have been retold countless times and are easy to find: *Rumplestiltskin,* the German tale, and *Tom Tit Tot,* the English version. Both stories involve the search for a name in exchange for a favor. Here are other name-related tales.

Davis, Virginia. *Simply Ridiculous.* Art by Russ Wilms. Kids Can, 1995. The humorous tale of a young man's ludicrous attempts to find a name for his son.

Hurwitz, Johanna. *The Adventures of Ali Baba Bernstein.* Art by Gail Owens. Morrow, 1985. David Bernstein finds seventeen people with his name in the Manhattan phone book.

Pitre, Felix. *Paco and the Witch.* Also in Spanish as *Paco y la Bruja.* Art by Christy Hale. Lodestar, 1995. A Puerto Rican variant of *Rumplestiltskin* with Spanish vocabulary.

Rylant, Cynthia. *The Old Woman Who Named Things.* Art by Kathryn Brown. Harcourt, 1996. An old woman is reluctant to give a name to the stray dog that visits her.

Rain

I couldn't resist. I bought one of those rain sticks the first time I saw a display in a department store gift shop. Now that I had one, however, I wondered, how I could I use it in the library? Read a book about rain and rain sticks and demonstrate how to make rain, of course.

Soon after my purchase, I met a storytelling couple in Sanibel, Florida, who offered me the perfect story to use with a rain stick. In fact, they had two stories. One gives the origin of the rain stick, and the other is a participation story. Both can be highlighted with hand-crafted rain sticks.

Craft a Rain Stick

The first rain stick I made used a tube mailer from the post office and a pound of nails. I spent time pounding the nails into the tube to catch beans and cause a racket as they tumbled through. I had fun making it, but I'm not sure how many children I could supervise while they played with hammer and nails.

After I showed my rain stick at a series of seminars, I received a number of suggestions about how to make a better, simpler rain stick. I've experimented with a variety of these ideas, and here is my favorite rain stick.

Supplies

one empty potato chip can with a plastic reusable cover
    for each rain stick

1/2 cup dry beans for each rain stick

paints or sticky-backed paper to decorate the can

10"-long piece of aluminum foil for each rain stick

    Plan ahead to collect enough cans for your group.
Don't feel compelled to eat 30 cans of potato chips.
Instead, display a sign on your bulletin board asking for
empty cans. They will come. In fact, years later people will
still be sending you cans. Tennis ball cans work. So do
empty paper towel tubes, but you will have
to tape both ends after you have filled the
tubes.

    Any type of beans work: split peas,
red beans, lima beans, rice, popcorn ker-
nels. Many packaged food items will work.
Experiment with what kind of bean you
prefer and about the amount you prefer.

Beans

Crumpled
aluminum
foil

1.

Preparation

Tell children to crush the aluminum foil
gently and stuff it lengthwise into the tube.
Have them drop a handful of beans into
the can and close the tube or can at both
ends (1). Now the rain stick is ready to
decorate on the outside with contact paper
or paint (2).

    Easy? Yes. And surprisingly good
enough to eat. I took my potato chip rain
stick all the way around the world to show
and tell at an international school in
Surabaya, Indonesia. I carefully laid out my materials to

2. Cover both
ends and
decorate
outside.

present to the children the next day. In the morning I found that the top of the rain stick had been gnawed through, and there were fewer beans and more holes in the foil. An Indonesian mouse had enjoyed a meal of my rain stick!

Share a Story

After you tell this story, show the rain stick and listen to the sound. Explain how different cultures believed in various traditions to help the spirits bring about rain. This legend explains how the rain stick came to be.

The Warrior Who Frightened the Evil One

Bert MacCarry

In a village on the banks of the Amazon River there lived a young boy. The other boys teased him because he was neither strong nor brave. He tried to keep up with the other boys, but he often lagged behind.

One moonless night, the boy met the Evil One by the side of the river. The boy knew of Evil One's mischief, but he also knew that this Evil One could grant requests.

"Please, sir," asked the boy. "I would like to be a valiant warrior. I will give you anything that you ask in return, if you will only grant my wish."

The Evil One said he would grant the boy's request in return for his soul. The boy thought his soul a small price to pay for becoming a brave warrior, so he agreed to the bargain. With time, the boy grew to be a respected chief in the village.

Many years passed. The chief had almost forgotten the bargain he had made with the Evil One.

He was quite elderly when the Evil One came to the village and asked to see the chief.

"I have come for your soul," Evil One said to the chief.

"Yes, yes," the chief said. "I remember, but may I have just one more day to prepare for my death? I would like to die with my own war club."

The Evil One granted the Chief's last request.

The next morning at daybreak the old chief went into the jungle and chose a stout bamboo-like tree. He cut it down and trimmed off the branches. He scraped out most of the spongy material from inside the tree trunk.

Then the chief poured sharp spines from another tree into the cylinder. He hammered the sharp spines into the log with a stone and plugged the opening on either end with clay. The stick now looked like a war club.

The old man returned to his hut. He put the stick against the wall and waited for the arrival of his visitor.

Early the next morning the Evil One arrived to collect the chief's soul. He walked into the hut and

saw what he thought was the old man's war club
leaning against the wall. The Evil One lifted the
club ready to kill the old man and collect his soul.
But a strange thing happened. Pine needles fell
through the spines of the log, making a thunderous
sound.

This was not a war club, the Evil One thought.
It must be some sort of demon ready to kill me.
Dropping the club, the Evil One ran from the old
man's hut.

The chief died many years later of old age.
During his last years he often picked up the war
club and turned it this way and that way, enjoying
the sounds of jungle rain.

Before you tell this story, divide your group into
four smaller groups. Assign each group a sound to make.
The four groups are frogs, ravens, coyotes, and the drums
of the Hopi people. Demonstrate and practice together
the sound each group should make. Give each group a
hand signal that you will use to indicate when they are to
start and stop their sound in the story. This is particularly
important with young children, who are eager to help but
find it difficult to quiet themselves without clear guide-
lines.

Tell the story, using a rain stick at the end of the
story. Help children make their own rain sticks. Tell the
story a second time. Now let the children shake their rain
sticks at the end of the story. What a storm!

The Frog

Bert MacCarry

Many years ago in a Hopi village in the territory of
Arizona there was a drought. No rain had fallen for

many weeks. The rivers were dry. The animals found no water to drink.

A little frog sitting on the bank of the dry riverbed said to himself, "I wonder if the Rain God has fallen asleep and forgotten to make it rain. Perhaps if I make a lot of noise I could wake him up." He began to croak, "Ribbit, Ribbit, Ribbit."

The other frogs heard him. "Why are you making so much noise?" they asked.

The little frog answered, "I think the Rain Spirit has fallen asleep and forgotten to make rain. I'm making a lot of noise so that he will wake up."

"We would like to help," said the other frogs. And they began to croak. (Signal frogs in the audience to help with "Ribbit, Ribbit, Ribbit.")

A raven flew over the dry river bed and heard the frogs croaking. "Why are you making so much noise?" the raven called to them. After the frogs explained, the raven said, "I would like to help." He shrieked a loud "Caw, Caw, Caw."

Other ravens said they would help too. They all began to caw. (Signal ravens in the audience to help with "Caw, Caw, Caw.")

A coyote in the desert heard the disturbance and called to the ravens flying overhead, "Why are you making so much noise?" The ravens explained the situation.

The coyote said, "I would like to help." He began to howl, "Ow-oo, Ow-oo, Ow-oo."

Other coyotes asked, "Why are you making so much noise?" The coyote explained, and the coyotes said, "We would like to help." They howled, "Ow-oo, Ow-oo, Ow-oo." (Coyotes in audience help with "Ow-oo, Ow-oo, Ow-oo.")

High on the cliffs, the villagers heard the noise from the frogs, ravens, and coyotes. "What is all the noise?" they asked.

When the animals explained, the people said, "We would like to help." They brought out their drums, dressed in their best dress, and began to chant and dance. (Signal Hopi drummers in the audience to help with "Drum, Drum, Drum.")

(Shake the rain stick.) Soon it began to rain. It rained and rained and rained. The Hopi and coyotes and ravens and frogs danced with joy. (Signal all the groups to make their sounds.)

They will always remember how one little frog can make a difference. Ribbit, Ribbit, Ribbit. (Signal all to be quiet except the frogs.)

Share a Book

Rain

Bauer, Caroline Feller. *Rainy Day.* Harper, 1986. Stories, poems, and activities featuring rain.

Bogacki, Tomek. *Cat and Mouse in the Rain.* Art by the author. Farrar, Strauss, 1997. Cat and mouse are warned by their families not to play together, but they enjoy romping in the rain and meeting a frog.

Bond, Ruskin. *Binya's Blue Umbrella.* Art by Vera Rosenberry. Boyds Mill, 1995. In this charming short novel, Binya is the envy of the village with her blue umbrella.

Branley, Franklyn M. *Down Comes the Rain.* Art by James Graham Hale. Harper, 1997. This simple story from the Let's Read and Find Out series explains the phenomenon of rain.

Calhoun, Mary. *Flood.* Art by Erick Ingraham. Morrow, 1997. Sarajean's family experiences the Midwest floods of 1993.

Compton, Patricia A. *The Terrible Eek.* Art by Sheila Hamanaka. Simon, 1991. The family talks about what frightens them during a rainstorm.

Dundon, Caitlin. *The Yellow Umbrella.* Art by Sandra Speidel. Simon, 1994. Umbrellas come in rainbow colors.

Lauber, Patricia. *Hurricanes.* Scholastic, 1996. Informational picture book format.

Lesser, Carolyn. *Storm on the Desert.* Art by Ted Rand. Harcourt, 1997. Experience the color and sound of a poetic desert storm.

Martin, Bill, Jr. *Listen to the Rain.* Art by James Endicott. Holt, 1988. Mood poem to share aloud.

Widman, Christine. *The Willow Umbrella.* Art by Catherine Stock. Macmillan, 1993. Two girls walk on a rainy day.

Rock Art

I now live in Bangladesh, a country that has very few rocks or stones. Since stone is used to build roads and buildings, the Bangladeshis form their own stone by making bricks and then pounding them by hand into small "stones."

Stones are special elsewhere in the world, too. Besides their many uses for construction, stones have been crafted into animals, insects, and rock gardens.

Perhaps some people in your group have stone collections, or they found a stone worth keeping. Ask them to think of how this stone might figure into a story. Is the stone a magic pebble that will grant wishes? Could it act as a symbol for a secret society? Or is a picture that is painted on the rock a hidden message to a friend?

Craft a Rock

Supplies

a rock for each crafter

paints (acrylics work well) and paint brushes

paper or felt cut-outs

scissors

craft glue

Preparation

The first thing you will need are rocks. Try to take your group for a walk so children can choose their own rocks. If you live in a big city, this may be a problem. I have found it difficult to pick up rocks in Miami Beach. We have lots of sand.

Garden shops will sell you pebbles, stones, and rocks. Another option is to wait until you go on a vacation and carry home enough rocks from your hikes in the woods to give to your group. Try to find stones that have at least a 1-1/2" surface for decorating. If finding rocks is impossible, provide each member of the group with a cut-out shape of a rock or make rocks of clay. (See page 126 "Sculpt a Book Character" and page 115, "Worms" for homemade clay recipes.)

Display sample rocks, including a rock ladybug, that you have decorated with various art materials. Encourage children to experiment with painting faces or designs, adding paper or felt to make figures, and gluing several stones together. If you have many rocks, construct a miniature fence, house, or village with the collection. Spread craft glue in between the stones as mortar.

Another group project could be an indoor rock garden. Arrange a group of stones into a pleasing pattern in a shoe box. Stand your favorite books in the rock garden and bolster them with larger rocks. Then the rock garden becomes a book exhibit as well as decoration.

Share a Poem

Lucky Ladybugs!
Charles Ghigna

The latest craft
That I like best
Is painting ladybugs
On rocks.

I gather stones
Down by the creek
Then bring them home
Inside a box.

I set them in
The morning sun
Until they are
All dry.

When I am finished
Painting them
They look like they
Could fly!

Before I start
To paint each one
I take my time
To look

At pictures
Of real ladybugs
That live inside
My book!

Share a Book

Rocks

Gans, Roma. *Let's Go Rock Collecting.*
Art by Holly Keller. Harper,
1997. A rock book about
what and how to collect.

Hooper, Meredith. *The Pebble in My Pocket.* Art by Chris
Coady. Viking, 1996. This story follows a pebble
from its creation 480 million years ago until you
pick it up and put it in your pocket.

Ladybugs

Bernhard, Emery. *Ladybug.* Art by Durga Bernhard.
Holiday, 1992. The life cycle of a ladybug is
explored.

Carle, Eric. *The Grouchy Ladybug.* Art by the author.
Harper, 1977. A ladybug meets a variety of animals
and is ready to challenge each one.

Fischer-Nagel, Heiderose, and Andreas Fischer-Nagel. *Life
of the Ladybug.* Illustrated with photographs that
show the life cycle of a ladybug.

Snakes

Snakes are always fascinating to children, especially if not everyone has to hug them. Share aloud the poem by Mary Ann Hoberman. Make these two types of snakes together. Read the poem again while the snakes dance to the words.

Craft a Dancing Snake

COILED SNAKE

Supplies

8-1/2" x 11" colored photocopy paper

scissors for each child

art supplies of choice

needle and thread (optional)

Match the bottom edge of the paper with the left side of the paper. Fold and cut off the top section, leaving an 8-1/2" x 8-1/2" square. Cut off the corners, so you now have a circle.

Begin cutting a spiral into the circle at the outer edge, gradually cutting away from the last circle so the strip is about 3/4" wide (1). Cut around and around until you reach the center. Leave a little wider section in the center for a face. Add features to the snake's head and body with art materials of your choice.

You may want to demonstrate for your group. Then they can follow what you have done. For children who may have difficulty controlling the scissors, you may want to photocopy the circular lines to cut on the paper.

Thread the needle with a knot at one end. Pull the thread through the head. This snake can wrap around the arms or dance suspended from the thread (2).

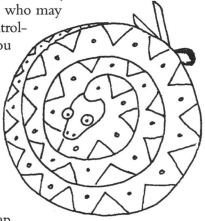

1. Cut a spiral into the circle, starting at the outer edge and leaving a wider section in the center for a face. Decorate your snake.

2. Thread a needle with a knot at one end. Pull thread through the head. This is how the snake can dance.

CATSTEP SNAKE

Supplies

2 different colored strips of paper, each about 1" wide
and 2' long (You can use photocopy, construction,
or wrapping paper or adding machine tape.)

colored scrap paper

glue

scissors

art materials of your choice

Preparation

To make your sample, lay the end of one strip over the
end of the other to form a right angle. Glue these ends
together (1).

Fold the bottom strip up over the top strip at the
glued end (2). Continue to fold whichever strip is on
the bottom over the top strip, forming a layer of folded
squares, until you come to the end of the paper (3).

Cut a paper snake head and tongue from the scrap
paper, and glue them to one end of the snake (4). Suggest that children write the title of their favorite book

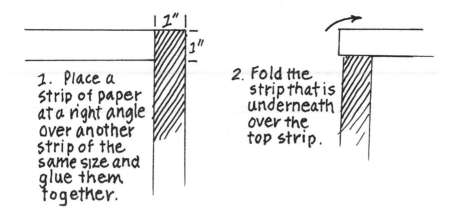

1. Place a strip of paper at a right angle over another strip of the same size and glue them together.

2. Fold the strip that is underneath over the top strip.

or a special message on the body of their snake, allotting one word for each fold. They can also decorate their snake in exciting colors and patterns. To keep their snakes from unraveling, glue the front and back ends together.

3. keep folding the bottom strip over the top strip until the paper is used up.

4. From scraps of paper, cut a head, a tail, and a snake tongue.

Share a Poem

Round and Round

Mary Ann Hoberman

Round and round in loops of gold
The silent snake creeps up the hill
Behold its zigzag coils unfold
Perfectly moving
Yet perfectly still

Share a Story

Snake Charmer's Rice

Caroline Feller Bauer

Sanyu loved to play his flute. At first his father was pleased with the lilting sounds that echoed through the walls of his home when his son practiced. However, now it was time for the son to join the father's rice distribution business.

Sanyu obediently spent time with the workers in the fields. He attended classes to help his father with the accounting, and he visited customers a day's walk from his home.

But Sanyu really didn't want to be in the rice business. He wanted to play the flute. Whenever Sanyu could steal some time from work, he brought his flute out of his back pocket and played.

One night, returning from a visit to a merchant in a distant town, the wind began to blow and rain whipped his face. Seeking shelter, Sanyu ran into

a cave by the side of the road. Exhausted and wet, he fell asleep on the floor of the cave. In the morning he awoke to find himself surrounded by a family of snakes. Their tongues darted out at Sanyu, and they slithered close to him.

Fearing for his life, Sanyu took the flute from his back pocket and prepared to use it as a weapon. A gentle man, he couldn't bring himself to kill even a snake. Instead, he played a quiet song on his flute. The snakes stopped moving and began to listen attentively. Sanyu picked up the beat, playing a dance tune. Now the snakes began to move in rhythm with the music.

They swayed to the beat and slithered in time to the music. As he played, Sanyu marched from the cave with the snakes behind him. When Sanyu returned to his father's house, the snakes were still dancing behind him.

"Father," said Sanyu. "I have tried to be a good son and become a rice expert, but unfortunately I still feel that I must follow my ambition and become a musician."

Sanyu's father wasn't listening. He was mesmerized by the snakes now curled behind his son.

"Son," whispered the father. "Don't move! There are at least 20 snakes behind you."

"I know, father," Sanyu said. "The snakes love my music. Watch this."

Sanyu took the flute from his back pocket and began to play. The snakes uncoiled themselves and started to dance.

Sanyu's father stared at the snakes and his son. He broke into a grin. "You've got it! The world's most amazing advertising idea for our rice. Yes!

Yes! Travel with your flute and snakes to each customer. Offer a concert in each village. We will rename our firm the *Snake Charmer's Rice.*"

Sanyu and his snakes were a great success. Snake Charmer's Rice sold well throughout the region. Sanyu could easily have hired others to travel and play the flute for the snakes. But he loved the snakes, and he loved being a musician.

Share a Book

Snakes

Cannon, Janell. *Verdi.* Art by the author. Harcourt, 1997. Verdi, a young python, is reluctant to grow up and become a boring old snake.

Dewey, Jennifer Owings. *Rattlesnake Dance.* Art by the author. Boyds Mill, 1997. Dewey gives the reader facts about rattlesnakes while relating her own experiences with snakes.

Ling, Mary, and Mary Atkinson. *The Snake Book.* Photos by Frank Greenaway and Dave King. Dorling Kindersley, 1997. Wow! These snakes jump off the page in double-spread photographs with an oversize format. Double-wow!

McNulty, Faith. *A Snake in the House.* Art by Ted Rand. Scholastic, 1994. A realistic story about a snake lost in a house.

Noble, Trinka Hakes. *The Day Jimmy's Boa Ate the Wash.* Art by Steven Kellogg. Dial, 1980. Also *El Día Que la Boa de Jimmy se Comío la Ropa,* Spanish edition. Dial, 1997. A field trip is not boring when a boa comes along.

Story Math

In children's literature there are untold stories related to math: counting books, money books, and now a groundswell of math function books. Each comes alive with hands-on crafts.

Craft a Stand-up Leopard

Encourage children to tell Leopard math to their families using their stand-up leopards as models: Have them count the number of spots they draw on their leopards while in small groups and count together.

Supplies

a sheet of 8 1/2" x 11" construction paper
    or poster paper
scissors
marking pen
2 different colors of signal dots (available
    at stationery stores)

Preparation

Prepare enough leopard sample patterns for your group. Pass out a sheet of paper to each child, and tell children to fold the paper lengthwise. Have them copy the pattern onto the edge of the paper and cut around the outline (1). Then children can unfold the paper and turn up the ears (2). The outside is ready to decorate with marking pen for the features and signal dots for the body (3).

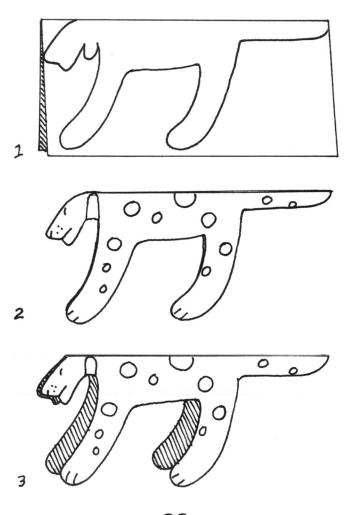

Share a Story

Children love to participate in stories. Insert group counting at the appropriate places.

Leopard Math

Caroline Feller Bauer

Leopard was proud of his spots, and he enjoyed showing them off. He would stroll by the river turning this way and that, hoping for an admiring glance. He liked it even better when one of the animals complimented him on his fine spots.

One bright sunny day, Leopard paraded in front of the river. The water reflected his spots and Leopard spent several minutes admiring himself.

"My spots are particularly outstanding today," he said.

Leopard was so enamored with his spots that he thought he would count them to see how many he had. He counted the spots on this right leg. (All together: "One, two, three, four, five.")

He counted the spots on his left leg. (All

together: "One, two, three, four, five.")

He lost count as he tried to count the spots on his chest. (Count to ten all together.)

And, of course, even though he turned this way and that way, he couldn't quite see to count the spots on his back.

Other animals at the river kept their distance from the lordly Leopard.

"Hello!" Leopard shouted. "As you can see I have many, many spots. I'm trying to determine exactly how many. Would someone please come and count them for me?"

Antelope wanted to please Leopard. "I'll try, sir," he said. Unfortunately, Antelope couldn't count beyond three. (Together.) "One, two, three. One two three," he said.

"Enough!" Leopard ordered. "I have more than three spots. Who else would like to try?"

Hippo thought she would like to try counting the spots. She stayed in the river half submerged and tried to count by fives. (Together.) "Five, ten, fifteen."

Hippo found a good, efficient way to count: by fives. Unfortunately, she couldn't count past 15, and even she knew that there were more than 15 spots on Leopard.

"Enough of this nonsense," shouted Leopard losing his temper. "I want my spots counted now or there will be trouble."

The animals by the river shrank back into the jungle. They feared Leopard when he was angry. One animal proved braver than the others, however. This was Rabbit. He knew he could run fast and hopefully escape if Leopard started to chase him.

"Sir," Rabbit said bowing low. "I know exactly how many spots you have."

"Good," Leopard said. "You may begin counting."

"Sir, I don't have to count," Rabbit replied. "I know exactly how many spots you have without counting."

"And how many is that?" asked Leopard.

"You have two spots," Rabbit answered.

"Two spots!" Leopard yelled. "Anyone can see that I have more than two spots."

"No sir," Rabbit explained. "You have two spots: light spots and dark spots."

"How clever you are, Rabbit. You are right. I have light spots and dark spots," Leopard agreed, turning this way and that way to admire himself in the river.

Rabbit grinned and hopped to the other side of the river. Clever Rabbit.

The Leopard's Daughter

Caroline Feller Bauer

Leopard's daughter was beautiful. She had a good sense of humor and was gentle and kind. When she was old enough to marry, many flocked to court her.

Leopard wanted his daughter to marry, but he wanted to make sure that he chose the right husband for his only daughter. Yet Leopard was sensitive to the feelings of others. He hesitated to choose one suitor over another because he didn't want to hurt anyone's feelings.

Then Leopard had a brilliant idea. He would hold a contest. Anyone who wanted to marry his daughter could enter the contest, and the winner would be his daughter's husband. Leopard felt proud of himself. What a good idea!

The next day Leopard sent out a proclamation announcing the contest to all the animals. A celebration feast would be part of the day's events.

On the day of the feast, a large crowd of animals assembled for the contest. Each suitor hoped to win the young leopard's hand in marriage. After everyone ate, Leopard rose to announce the rules of the contest.

"Each contestant will toss a spear into the air," he said. "Before it hits the ground, the contestant must count to ten."

The animals smiled smugly to themselves. The contest sounded easy. Anyone could toss a spear in the air and count to ten before it landed.

"And," Leopard continued, "I would like each of you to dance before you throw the spear into the air. I want to make sure that my daughter will marry a clever as well as an honest and caring husband. Dance the Dance of War to show that you will defend my daughter from any enemies and also dance the Dance of Peace to show that you care about the earth and all its living creatures."

Again everyone nodded. Surely the contest would be won by the first contestant. It all sounded so easy.

"I'll be first," Elephant volunteered. He stepped into the circle of animals. Gracefully, he danced the

Dance of War and the Dance of Peace.
Everyone applauded. Taking the spear
from Leopard, Elephant threw the
spear into the air as high as he could
and quickly counted: "One, two,
three . . . ." But before he got to four,
the spear fell back to earth.
Embarrassed, Elephant sat
down muttering to himself.

The next contestant was
mighty Buffalo. Confidently, he swaggered into the
center of the circle of animals. He wasn't quite as
graceful as Elephant, but he competently danced
the Dance of War and the Dance of Peace.

Once again the animals applauded. Now, grip-
ping the spear tightly and grunting with all his
strength, Buffalo hurled the spear as high as he was
able straight into the air. Quickly he counted: "One,
two, three, four . . . ." But by the time he got to
five, the spear had landed on the ground.
Frustrated, Buffalo sat down. "The task is not as
easy as it looks," Buffalo grumbled.

"The task seems impossible," cried the other
animals. "Leopard is playing a trick on us."

Leopard looked worried. He hadn't meant to set
such an impossible task. He wanted his daughter
married. If Elephant and Buffalo had failed, no one
else would even dare to try to win his daughter.

"May I have a turn now?" a voice whispered.

Everyone looked at the center of the circle.
There stood the tiny Dwarf Antelope. The other
animals giggled. Surely, the little antelope could not
succeed where the larger more powerful animals
had failed.

Leopard prided himself on being fair. "Yes.
Antelope, it is your turn now. Good Luck."

The animals stopped laughing, but still they smiled. Dwarf Antelope didn't have any chance at all to win the contest, but it was a nice day. They would enjoy his dancing since Dwarf Antelope was known to be nimble and dainty in his movements.

Dwarf Antelope grasped the spear. First he danced the Dance of War, showing that he would protect his wife from all enemies. Then with rhythmic grace he danced the Dance of Peace, demonstrating that he cared for the earth and all its living creatures.

Now with all his force he threw the spear into the air. It didn't go very high, but it went straight. Dwarf Antelope shouted, "Five plus five are ten!" and caught the spear as it fell to earth.

"Hooray!" The animals shouted. "Little Dwarf Antelope has succeeded."

Leopard was pleased. He thought it quite clever of Dwarf Antelope to think of another way to count.

Leopard's daughter married Dwarf Antelope. She danced the Dance of Love for her new husband.

Share a Book

Math

Adler, David A. *Fraction Fun*. Art by Nancy Tobin. Holiday, 1996. The concept of fractions is explored with pizza, money, and a paper plate.

Demi. *One Grain of Rice: A Mathematical Folktale.* Art by the author. Scholastic, 1997. Rani, a village girl, teaches the raja a lesson in mathematical progression.

Leedy, Loreen. *Mission Addition.* Art by the author. Holiday, 1994. Six stories featuring addition problems and Miss Prime, the hippo teacher, and her students. See also Fraction Action, 1994.

McGrath, Barbara Barbieri. *The M & M's Book.* Art by the author. Charlesbridge, 1994. Candy pieces illustrate colors, numbers, shapes, and sets.

McMillan, Bruce. *Jelly Beans for Sale.* Photos by the author. Scholastic, 1996. Children are shown selling jelly beans. How many can you buy with 10 pennies?

Murphy, Stuart J. *A Pair of Socks.* Art by Lois Ehlert. Harper, 1996. An introduction to matching patterns in the Mathsmart series.

Pinczes, Elinor. *Arctic Fives Arrive.* Art by Holly Berry. Houghton Mifflin, 1996. Arctic animals arrive by fives to watch the wonder of the northern lights.

Leopards

Hadithi, Mwenye. *Baby Baboon.* Art by Adrienne Kennaway. Little, 1993. Lazy leopard captures Baby Baboon.

Scott, Jonathan. *The Leopard Family Book.* Illustrated with photos. Picture Book, 1991. Photo essay shows the leopard up close and personal.

Souhami, Jessica. *The Leopard's Drum: An Asante Tale from West Africa.* Art by the author. Little Brown, 1995. Nyame, the Sky-God, offers a reward to the animal who brings him Osebo, the leopard's magnificent drum.

Whales
and the Sea

After listening to the following story, "Living in W'ales," your children will enjoy making their own whale that can swallow a little girl, a dog, a bed, and more.

Craft a Whale

Supplies

sheet of computer paper for each person

scissors

stapler or white glue

art supplies of your choice

cotton balls (optional)

Preparation

To make your sample, fold the paper in half. Draw the outline of a whale on one side of the folded paper. Cut through the two thicknesses of paper to make two identical whale shapes (1).

Staple (or glue) the whale around the outside, leaving the whale's wide mouth open. Decorate the whale (2).

Then draw, cut, and decorate shapes for the whale to swallow. There will be enough scrap paper left after cutting the whale to make the objects (3).

Stuff some cotton balls deep into the whale to keep the two sides apart. The cotton will also serve as beds for the shapes that may include a dog and sleepy girl from the story. Have children put a dab of glue on the back of their shapes before placing them on the cotton (4).

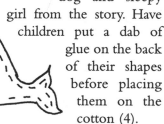

Craft a Paper Plate Aquarium

Tell students to make a paper plate aquarium to take home to their parents. It's colorful and much less trouble than a real aquarium.

Supplies

two styrofoam dinner plates	scissors
brightly colored paper	cellophane tape
yarn	stapler
plastic wrap	

Preparation

For younger groups or if you have too little time, you may want to precut plastic wrap circles to cover the plastic plates. Each child will need one circle. You can also cut the center out of one plate for each participant, leaving a 1-1/2" border (1).

To prepare your sample, cover the hole of the aquarium (the cut-out plastic plate) as tightly as possible with plastic wrap. As you probably know, plastic wrap wants to adhere to everything. Prepare the border of the plate to hold the "see-through glass" of the aquarium by putting pieces of tape on the border (2). Take the plastic wrap in both hands and press from the center out to fix the wrap tightly onto the plate. Tape down. If necessary, trim the edges of the plastic, so they won't show. Set the plate aside.

Now you are ready to create your sea scene. Cut a variety of plants and coral from the colored paper and tape them to the inside edge of the second plate. I prefer tape because the plants will stand away from the plate enough to create a three-dimensional illusion (3).

Tape yarn to the back of each fish so the fish hang freely in between both plates (4). Tape the other end of the yarn to the top edge of the back of the plate. Then staple the two plates together and trim any excess yarn (5). Leave enough time for children to share their aquariums. This project also makes a colorful display with books about the sea.

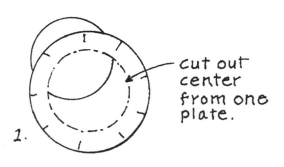

1. cut out center from one plate.

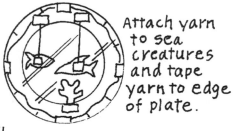

2. Plastic wrap

Tape

3. Cut out fish shapes and tape yarn to back.

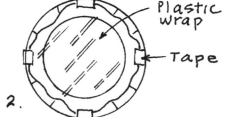

4. Attach yarn to sea creatures and tape yarn to edge of plate.

staple the
two plates
together
and trim excess
yarn and
plastic wrap.

5.

Share a Story

Richard Hughes' story has just the right amount of silliness to appeal to your group's funny bones. Since you will probably be telling or reading the story aloud, children will not see the joke of the spelling of W'ales and whales. Therefore, you may want to point it out by showing a picture of a whale and a map that shows where Wales is located. Understanding the distinction is part of the joke.

Living in W'ales

Richard Hughes

Once there was a man who said he didn't like the sort of houses people lived in, so he built a model village. It was not really like a model village at all, because the houses were all big enough for real people to live in, and he went about telling people to come and live in W'ales.

There was also living in Liverpool a little girl who was very nice. So when all the people went off with the man to live in W'ales, she went with them. But the man walked so fast that presently some of them got left behind. The ones who were left behind were the little girl, an Alsatian dog, a very cross old lady in a bonnet and black beads, who was all stiff, but had a nice husband, who was left behind, too.

So they went along till they came to the sea; and in the sea was a whale. The little girl said, "That was what he meant, I suppose, when he talked about living in W'ales. I expect the others are inside: or if not, they are in another one. We had better get in this one."

So they shouted to know if they might come in, but the whale didn't hear them. The nice husband said that if that was what living in W'ales meant, he would rather go back to Liverpool; but the horrid old lady said, "Nonsense! I will go and whisper in its ear."

But she was very silly, and so instead of whispering in its ear, she went and tried to whisper in its blowhole. Still the whale didn't hear; so she got very cross and said, "None of this nonsense, now! Let us in at once! I won't have it, do you hear? I simply won't stand it!" and she began to stir in his blowhole with her umbrella.

So the whale blew, like an enormous sneeze, and blew her right away up into the sky on top of the water that he blew out of his hole, and she was never seen again. So then the nice husband went quietly back to Liverpool.

But the little girl went to the whale's real ear, which was very small and not a bit like his blowhole, and she whispered into it, "Please, nice whale, we would so like to come in, if we may, and live inside." Then the whale opened his mouth, and the little girl and the Alsatian dog went in.

When they got right down inside, of course, there was no furniture. "He was quite right," said the little girl. "It is certainly not a bit like living in a house."

The only thing in there was a giant's wig that the whale had once eaten. So the little girl said, "This will do for a door mat." So she made it into a door mat, and the Alsatian dog went to sleep on it.

When he woke up again, he started to dig holes; and of course, it gave the whale most terrible pains to have holes dug by such a big dog in his inside, so he went up to the top of the water and shouted to the captain of a ship to give him a pill. On board the ship there was a cold dressed leg of mutton that the captain was tired of, so he thought, "That will make a splendid pill to give the whale." So he threw it to the whale, and the whale swallowed it; and when it came tobogganing down the whale's throat, the Alsatian dog, who was very hungry, ate it, and stopped digging holes; and when the dog stopped digging holes, the whale's pain went away. So he said, "Thank you" to the captain: "That was an excellent pill."

The captain was very surprised that his pill had made the whale well again so soon; he had really only done it to get rid of the cold mutton.

But the poor little girl wasn't so lucky as the Alsatian dog. He had a door mat to sleep on and something to eat. But there was no bed, and the little girl couldn't sleep without a bed to sleep on, and had nothing to eat. This went on for days and days.

Meanwhile the whale began to get rather worried about them. He had swallowed them without thinking much about it; but he soon began to wonder what was happening to them, and whether they were comfortable. He knew nothing at all

about little girls. He thought she would probably
want something to eat by now, but he didn't know
at all what. So he tried to talk down into his own
inside, to ask her. But that is very difficult; at any
rate he couldn't do it. The words all came out
instead of going in.

So he swam off to the tropics, where he knew a
parrot, and asked him what to do. The parrot said it
was quite simple, and flew off to an island where
there was a big snake. He bit off its head and bit off
its tail, and then flew back to the whale with the
rest of it. He put most of the snake down the
whale's throat so that one end just came up out of
its mouth.

"There," he said, "now you have got a speaking
tube. You speak into one end of the snake, and the
words will go down it inside you."

So the whale said "Hallo" into one end of the
snake, and the little girl heard "Hallo" come out of
the other. "What do you want?" said the whale. "I
want something to eat," said the little girl. The
whale told the parrot, "She wants something to eat.
What do little girls eat?"

"Little girls eat rice pudding," said the parrot.
He had one in a big glass bowl, so he poured it
down the snake too, and it came down the other
end and the little girl ate it.

When she had eaten it she caught hold of her
end of the snake and called "Hallo!" up it.

"Hallo!" said the whale.

"May I have a bed?" said the little girl.

"She wants a bed," the whale said to the parrot.

"You go to Harrods for that," said the parrot,
"which is the biggest shop in London," and flew
away.

When the whale got to Harrods, he went inside.
One of the shopwalkers came up to him and

said, "What can I do for *you,*
please?" which sounded very
silly.
"I want a bed," said the
whale.
"Mr. Binks, BEDS!"
The shopkeeper
called out very loud
and then ran away. He
was terribly frightened,
because there had never
been a whale in the
shop before.

Mr. Binks the Bed Man came up and looked
rather worried.

"I don't know that we have got a bed that will
exactly fit you, sir," he said.

"Why not, silly?" said the whale. "I only want an
ordinary one."

"Yes, sir," said the bed man, "but it will have to
be rather a large ordinary one, won't it?"

"Of course not, silly," said the whale. "On the
contrary, it will have to be rather a small one."

He saw a very nice little one standing in a corner.

"I think that one will just about fit me," he said.

"You can have it if you like," said the Bed Man.
"But I think it's you who are the silly to think a
little bed like that will fit you!"

"I want it to fit me inside, of course," said the
whale, "not outside!—Push!" and he opened his
mouth.

So they all came and pushed, and sure enough it
just did fit him. Then he ate all the pillows and
blankets he could find, which was far more than
was needed really, and when it all got down inside,
the little girl made the bed and went to sleep on it.

So the whale went back to the sea. Now that the little girl and the Alsatian dog both had had something to eat and somewhere to sleep, they said: "The man was right; it really is much more fun living in W'ales than living in houses." So they stayed on.

P.S.—The parrot went on feeding them, not always on rice pudding.

Share a Book

Whales

Allen, Judy. *Whale*. Art by Tudor Humphries. Candlewick, 1992. A herd of whales rescues a mother and baby whale caught in an oil slick.

Carrick, Carol. *Whaling Days*. Art by David Frampton. Clarion, 1993. Woodcuts and text survey the history of whaling.

Davies, Nicola. *Big Blue Whale*. Art by Nick Maland. Candlewick, 1997. This book examines the life cycle of the blue whale in an attractive format that makes you want to dive into the ocean.

Gibbons, Gail. *Whales*. Art by the author. Holiday, 1991. Facts and drawings introduce whales to the reader.

Johnston, Tony. *Whale Song*. Art by Ed Young. Putnam, 1987. A whale counting book.

McMillan, Bruce. *Going on a Whale Watch*. Photos by the author. Scholastic, 1992. Minimal text accompanies color photographs of a whale-spotting voyage.

Ryder, Joanne. *Winter Whale*. Art by Michael Rothman. Morrow, 1991. This story investigates what it feels like to be a humpbacked whale.

Sheldon, Dyan. *The Whale's Song.* Art by Gary Blythe. Dial, 1990. Grandmother tells Lilly about the whales of her childhood.

Simon, Seymour. *Whales.* Photos. Harper, 1989. This nonfiction text explores the life of several species of whales.

Waters, John F. *Watching Whales.* Photos. Cobblehill, 1991. The story follows students on a field trip search for whales off Cape Cod.

The Sea

Farber, Norma. *I Swim in My Ocean.* Art by Elivia Savadier. Holt, 1997. The main character dreams about swimming through the ocean.

Gourley, Catherine. *Sharks! True Stories and Legends.* Illustrated with photos. Millbrook, 1996. An anthology of fact and legend featuring sharks.

Guiberson, Brenda Z. *Into the Sea.* Art by Alix Berenzy. Holt, 1996. A sea turtle travels on her life journey from beach to sea to beach.

Kovacs, Deborah, and Kate Madin. *Beneath Blue Waters: Meetings with Remarkable Deep-Sea Creatures.* Photos by Larry Madin. Viking, 1996. In this book you meet some of the weirder-looking creatures of the sea.

Livingston, Myra Cohn. *If You Ever Meet a Whale.* Art by Leonard Everett Fisher. Holiday, 1992. Poetry featuring whales accompanied by double-spread art.

Ryder, Joanne. *Shark in the Sea.* Art by Michael Rothman. Morrow, 1997. The story examines what it would be like to be a shark for a day.

Worms

As a child in Washington, D.C., I played with home-made clay on rainy days and made, as many children do . . . mostly worms, snakes, and pots.

Here is a traditional recipe for homemade clay. (Additional recipes for homemade clay are in the General Crafts section.) Let your students create worms and other clay characters from the following story, poems, and chants to "Show and Tell" the group.

Craft Kid's Clay Worms

A truly "homemade" concoction, this clay makes nice beads and, of course, worms. Making the clay is half the fun, and this recipe, unlike others later in the General Crafts section, requires no stove.

Supplies

1 cup flour

1/2 cup salt

1/2 cup warm water

bowl large enough for ingredients

1 tablespoon oil (optional for smoother clay)

food coloring (optional)

poster paints (optional)

Preparation

Either have children measure their own ingredients or measure the first three ingredients yourself. Add multiple amounts of ingredients for larger groups. Place ingredients in the bowl and have the children mix them until they are blended. This is the fun squishy, gooey part.

Adjust ingredient proportions, depending upon whether you prefer softer or harder clay. Once ingredients seem workable, let children roll their worms.

Clay can be colored with food coloring before it is sculpted or painted with poster paints after the masterpiece is completed. Remind children to work quickly or carefully wrap their unfinished project, as Kid's Clay dries fast if left unprotected.

Share or Act Out a Story

Marty's Worm

Caroline Feller Bauer

Marty skipped around the garden.
She picked up a flower and smelled it.
She picked up a ball and threw it.
She picked up a worm and
    dangled it between two
    fingers.

Marty skipped over to her dad
    and showed him the worm.
Marty's dad said, "Disgusting!"

Marty skipped over to her mom and
 showed her the worm.
Her mom said, "Unappetizing!"
Marty skipped over to her brother and showed him
 the worm.
Her brother said, "Yuck!"
Marty skipped over to her sister and showed her
 the worm.
Her sister said, "Distasteful!"

Marty skipped next door to show the worm to
 Mr. Ramirez.
Mr. Ramirez said, "Repulsivo!"

Marty skipped down the street to show the worm
 to the librarian.
The librarian said, "Repugnant!"

Marty sat down under a tree.
A robin sat next to her.
Quietly, Marty showed the robin the worm.
The robin said, "Yummy!" and ate the worm.

Share Some Poems

I Brought a Worm

Kalli Dakos

Jane brought a baseball bat
And a ball for sharing time.

But I brought a worm!

Rich brought a goldfish bowl
Without a goldfish.

But I brought a worm!

Worms

Lizzie brought an egg yolk
And an egg without a yolk.

But I brought a worm!

Joe brought an eraser shaped like a knife
And an olive sandwich.

But I brought a worm!

Jane showed us how to hit
The ball with the bat.

Rich put the class turtle
In the goldfish bowl.

Lizzy showed us how to prick an egg
And take the yolk out.

Joe tried to cut his sandwich
With his eraser knife.
But I ate the worm!
Right there in front of everyone
I ate the worm!
(It was a candy worm.)

Why I'm Glad I'm Not A Worm

Jeff Moss

I'd feel so blue
When people went, "Eeeyuuuuu!"

Two Gardeners
Douglas Florian

Tara planted tulip bulbs
And black-eyed Susan seed.
Peter planted light bulbs
So all the worms could read.

The Worm Song
Brod Bagert

Worms for breakfast
Worms for lunch
Worms for supper too,
Worms for Mom
Worms for Dad
And worms for me and you.

I cannot eat another worm
Please give me something new.
My stomach is real hungry
For a bowl of lizard stew.

Share a Worm Chant

Add the hand motions and sound effects as you chant this clever chant. Kids will love the surprise ending.

Sittin' on a Fence

Chewing on my bubble gum (Chomp. Chomp. Chomp.)
Playing with my yo-yo (Whee. Whee. Whee.)
When along came Herman the Worm.
And Herman was this big. (Show how big with your
two hands.)

And I said, "Herman, how come you're this big?"
He said, "I ate my mother."
(Repeat adding father, sister, brother, Aunt Myrtle, etc.
Show with your hands that Herman is getting longer
and longer. On the last verse Herman returns to
being a smaller size.)

And I asked, "How come you're this big?" (Show how
small with your hands.)
He said, "I burped."

Craft a Worm

ATTENTION! ATTENTION!
The following idea might not appeal to you at
all. Feel free to shut your eyes and move onto
the next idea.

Years and years ago, and I'm not saying how many years,
I attended a summer camp in Maine. We were forbidden
to chew gum. (My nice mom sent me a pack and I kept
it hidden under a rock outside my cabin. It got quite sod-
den in a rainstorm. I chewed it anyway and survived.)
One rainy week, the counselors had run out of ideas to
keep us from mutiny, so they relented.

During our rainy day activities in the barn, we were
each given a piece of gum to chew and enjoy. To keep us
from keeping the gum for another day, they devised an art
contest. Each child was given a small sheet of paper and a
toothpick to use as a sculpting tool. We were asked to
sculpt something from the *chewed* gum. Sounds "gross,"
eh? But it was fun and some of the "clay" pieces were
masterpieces. I won a prize for making a quite ordinary
worm as my entry. I supposed everyone was given a prize.

My suggestion: Try it. Your children will remember the activity into adulthood. I have.

Or make your worms from paper (see snakes) or yarn. Braided snakes would be colorful, if not as tasty as chewing gum worms.

Share a Book

Worms

Carle, Eric. *The Very Hungry Caterpillar.* Art by the author. Putnam, 1981. This is the classic tale of a caterpillar with a large appetite.

Carroll, Lewis. *Alice's Adventures in Wonderland.* Art by John Tenniel. Putnam, 1963. Just a reminder: This classic has an intelligent caterpillar as a leading character.

Dahl, Roald. *James and the Giant Peach.* Art by Nancy Burket. Knopf, 1961. This is a novel-length story in which an earthworm and a silkworm accompany James on a journey inside a peach.

Davies, Gillian. *Why Worms?* Art by Robin Kramer. Wishing Well, 1989. A little boy draws worms, worms, worms.

Glaser, Linda. *Wonderful Worms.* Art by Loretta Krupinski. Millbrook, 1992. This informational essay describes the world of earthworms.

Rockwell, Thomas. *How to Eat Fried Worms.* Art by Emily McCully. Watts, 1973. To win a bet in this novel, Willie must eat fifteen worms in fifteen days.

Ross, Michael Elsohn. *Wormology.* Carolrhoda, 1996. The picture book covers introductory information about worms.

General Crafts

I still have the jigsaw puzzle I made in summer camp when I was nine. We used a jigsaw and real wood to make it. Here is a faster, easier way to craft a picture puzzle.

My Favorite Book Puzzle

Supplies

5" x 7" index card for each person

scissors

letter envelope for each person

art materials of your choice

Preparation

Ask each child to color one side of their card with a scene or character and write the title and author of their favorite book (1). Tell them to draw lines on the other side of the card to serve as puzzle piece outlines (2). Have children cut the pieces.

Put each child's puzzle pieces into an envelope with the child's name. Have kids exchange envelopes and put the puzzles together. Give children a chance to talk about the book represented on their puzzle.

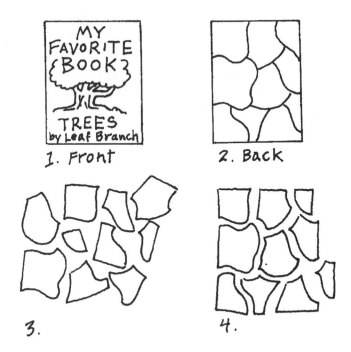

1. Front   2. Back

3.   4.

Share a Book

Mysteries

Mysteries are puzzles and children usually love them.

Clifford, Eth. *Flatfoot Fox and the Case of the Missing Schoolhouse.* Art by Brian Lies. Houghton, 1997. Principal Porcupine asks Detective Flatfoot Fox to find a missing building.

Cushman, Doug. *The ABC Mystery.* Art by the author. Harper, 1993. Discover the thieves as you follow Detective Inspector McGroom through the alphabet.

Monsell, Mary. *The Mysterious Cases of Mr. Pin.* Simon & Schuster, 1989. Ace penguin detective from the South Pole, Mr. Pin, solves mysteries in Chicago.

Skofield, James. *Detective Dinosaur.* Art by R. W. Alley. Harper, 1996. Five I Can Read stories about a silly detective and his clever sidekick Officer Pterodactyl.

Whatley, Bruce. *Detective Donut and the Wild Goose Chase.* Art by Rosie Smith. Harper, 1997. Detective Donut and Mouse search for Professor Drake, the missing archaeologist.

Yolen, Jane. *Piggins and the Royal Wedding.* Art by Jane Dyer. Harcourt, 1989. Piggins helps to solve the mystery of the missing wedding ring.

Box

On a visit to an international school in southeast Asia, I brought a large bag of carrot seeds. I wanted every child to go home with some seeds to grow their own carrots. Each child made a paper box to carry the seeds home.

This is another easy and quick craft that can be used for a number of programs. The directions are for one open box. If children make two boxes, they will have one that serves as a lid and fits over the other box. Two boxes fitted this way also make a block that can be decorated with library symbols, mottos, or book titles.

Here are some other uses for the boxes:

Suggest that children put into their boxes an object representing a story or poem.

Use the box to store slips of paper with book titles that have been read.

Collect vocabulary words and their definitions on slips of paper and store them in the box.

Make a guessing box. Put a book title in the box. Make up four clues to the identity of the book, and write or draw them on the four sides of the cube. Can the other participants in your group guess the title of the book?

Example:
I have a basket filled with goodies.

My grandmother lives in the forest.

I often wear a red cape.

I meet a stranger on the way to visit Grandma.

Title: "Little Red Riding Hood"

Craft a Paper Box

Supplies

sheet of computer paper cut into
an 8-1/2" x 8-1/2" square
(Keep the extra paper strip.)

scissors

art materials of your choice

tape or glue

Preparation

Have children decorate one side of
the square. Then fold the paper into
three equal parts horizontally (1). Open the paper and
fold the sheet vertically into three equal parts (2). Open
the paper again and you should see nine boxes.

Cut two slits on the folds framing the top center box
and two more for the bottom center box (3). Fold the two
top boxes inward, fold the top center box over them (4),
and glue or tape the side (5). Follow the same procedure
for the bottom center square, and tape or glue the sides in
place (6).

Hint: Use the extra paper strip to make a handle. This will turn your box into a basket.

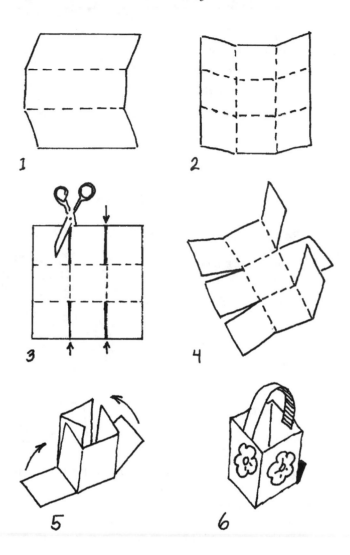

Sculpt a Book Character

About an hour out of Quito, Ecuador, there is a small village known for its bread sculpture. Five or six small shops line the main street and devote themselves to the sale of pins, napkin rings, baskets, and representations of religious figures, animals, and vehicles—all sculpted from homemade clay. Here I bought 100 little baskets with love birds perched on the side as favors for my daughter's wedding. They held the bird seed that we threw at the "just married" couple as they left the wedding.

Sculpting is part of many cultures. In some, the resulting figures bring a much-needed livelihood. In others, such as in the United States, children have the luxury of sculpting for pleasure.

Here are some traditional recipes for homemade clay, including bread dough clay from Ecuador. These recipes make small quantities for you to try at home. Double or triple the ingredients as your need dictates.

Have a clay party at home in your kitchen to try this selection of clay recipes. Choose the recipe you think will work best with your group and activity. If possible, prepare the clay as a group. Then suggest that students sculpt objects, characters, or scenes from a book to share with the group.

Craft Bread Dough Clay

Supplies

2 slices of white bread with the crusts removed

1 tablespoon white glue

Preparation

Rip and tear the bread into small pieces and mix with the glue. Use a fork because the mixture is too sticky to work with your hands until it is well mixed. If the mixture stays too sticky, work in more bread.

The gloss of this clay has a professional look. The dough dries out quickly, however, and must be used in one session. To add more gloss, use equal parts of white glue and water. Paint this mixture on the outside of the sculpture with a brush and allow it to dry for one to three days, depending on whether you live in Arizona (dry) or Florida (wet).

Craft Cornstarch Clay

Supplies

1 cup salt   1/2 cup cornstarch

1/3 cup water   1/4 cup cold water

Preparation

Heat the salt and water in a saucepan over medium heat for about four minutes. Remove the pan from the stove, and add the cornstarch and cold water. Stir until the clay thickens. Allow the pan to cool before handling the mixture.

You can make bowls and large animals with this recipe. Color the dough with food coloring before sculpting or with paints after your shapes dry.

Craft Class Clay

Supplies

1 cup flour   1 teaspoon vegetable oil

1 cup water   1/2 teaspoon cream of tartar

1/2 cup salt

Preparation

Mix all ingredients together in a saucepan over medium heat. Cool and you are ready to work.

This clay is my choice for schools, since it doesn't dry as quickly as the others. It can be stored for several days or even weeks. As with cornstarch clay, color with food coloring before modeling or paint your masterpiece when finished. Suggest that children paint their shape white as a base and let it dry. Then they can add other colors.

Door Knob Hanger

I get almost panicky if I find myself somewhere without anything to read. The books that my family and I carry at all times we call our "flood books." The tradition of always carrying a "flood book" began in Oregon where it rained a lot. No one wanted to be caught in a flood without a book to read. The flood book idea has extended to cover any print material that is carried as insurance against being stuck somewhere without something to read. Horrors!

We have learned to keep our clothes to a minimum when we travel, but we are not so disciplined about the books we tote around the world. The books in our travel library are usually piled on the hotel's television set. They are heavy to carry, and one would think that the weight would diminish as we read and discarded them, but we usually end up with the same amount of books or more as we travel. It's amazing that you can find books to buy almost anywhere.

In my children's and adult workshops, I often give away little address stickers that remind people to take their flood books with them. I purchased these from a stationery company. The point is to stick the sticker onto the door before you leave to remind yourself to always bring a flood book with you. Another form of reminder that travels well is a door knob hanger.

Craft a Flood Book Doorknob Hanger

Encourage children to bring a reminder back to the family in the form of a doorknob hanger. They can place the hanger on the front door, or make one for each member of the family to hang on their bedroom doors.

Supplies

scissors
art paper of your choice (construction paper makes a stiffer hanger)
art materials of your choice
glue (optional)
laminating machine or clear sticky-back paper (optional)

Preparation

Have children each cut a 4" x 10-1/2" strip of paper, or precut the strips. Suggest decorating them with a picture of someone reading a flood book, as in the sample. Make sure children add the words Remember Your Flood Book. In the center of the strip, have them cut a partial circle with slit on the top so the hanger fits around a doorknob.

> *Hint:* Instead of children drawing their own pictures, you can give them a printed doorknob hanger to color and possibly paste onto a strip of stiffer paper.

Laminating the finished hangers will make them look more professional.

Flying

Tell children to make an airplane that promotes their favorite book. Allow time to talk about the books and fly the finished planes.

Craft a Paper Plane

This is the classic paper plane. Follow directions shown in the illustrations.

Supplies

sheet of computer paper for each plane
art materials of your choice

Preparation

Fold the paper in half lengthwise (1).

Unfold the page and fold the top two points inward toward the center along dotted lines (2).

Fold the sides inward toward the center again along the dotted lines (3).

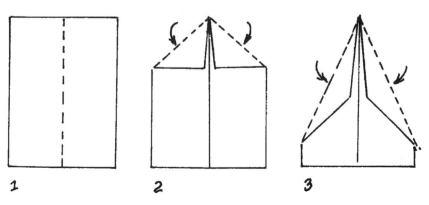

1   2   3

Turn the plane over and fold the sides inward to the
center along the dotted lines. The wings will meet
in the center (4).

Turn the plane over and fold in half to the center, tuck-
ing in any folds that may come loose (5).

Hold the plane from the underside fold and push the
wings back from center.

Decorate.

Fly!

Share a Book

Flying

Blackburn, Ken, and Jeff Lammers. *World Record Paper Airplane Kit.* World Record Airplane Company. 1270 Clearmont Street, NE Palm Bay, Florida 32905. Designs for 45 paper planes ready to fold, cut, and fly.

Brown, Don. *Ruth Law Thrills a Nation.* Art by the author. Ticknor/Houghton, 1993. In 1916, a young woman tries to fly from Chicago to New York in a single day.

Burleigh, Robert. *Flight: The Journey of Charles Lindbergh.* Art by Mike Wimmer. Putnam, 1991. Young Lindbergh flies across the Atlantic.

Davis, Meredith. *Up and Away!* Art by Ken Dubrowski. Mondo, 1997. Passengers, baggage handlers, and flight crew are followed on a flight.

Hart, Philip S. *Up in the Air: The Story of Bessie Coleman.* Carolrhoda, 1996. A biography of the first African-American woman in the United States to earn a pilot's license.

Lindbergh, Reeve. *Nobody Owns the Sky.* Art by Pamela Paparone. Candlewick, 1996. Bessie Coleman, who was black and a woman, was told she couldn't fly. She disagreed and said, "Nobody owns the sky."

Lobato, Arcadio. *Paper Bird.* Art by Emilio Urberuaga. Carolrhoda, 1993. Can a bird drawn on a piece of paper fly?

Magee, Doug, and Robert Newman. *Let's Fly from A to Z.* Photos. Cobblehill, 1992. Color photos show an airplane from take-off to landing.

Moser, Barry. *Fly!* Art by the author. Harper, 1993. An illustrated survey of the history of flight.

Provensen, Alice and Martin. *The Glorious Flight across the Channel with Louis Blériot, July 25, 1909*. Art by the authors. Louis flies across the English channel in 37 minutes.

Shea, George. *First Flight: The Story of Tom Tate and the Wright Brothers*. Art by Don Bolognese. Harper, 1997. Tom is there when the Wright brothers fly their first airplane in an I Can Read chapter book.

Siebert, Diane. *Plane Song*. Art by Vincent Nasta. Harper, 1993. Varieties of aircraft are described in verse accompanied by paintings.

Testa, Fulvio. *The Paper Airplane*. Art by the author. Holt, 1988. Fly away in your paper airplane.

Fortune Cookies

My husband, Peter, has conducted business in Asia for a number of years. Each time we visit Hong Kong or Taiwan, his agents try to outdo each other with elaborate banquets. I was astonished to discover that fortune cookies are an American invention. Once Peter's designer brought a bag of American fortune cookies all the way from Oregon to share with our Asian hosts. They were delighted.

Fortune cookies can be used to predict what book a child will read or to foretell the fortune of your participants. Diners can't eat the casing on these fortune cookies, but children might want to create fortunes to eat with a cookie.

Craft a Fortune Cookie

Supplies

colored construction paper or posterboard square 3" x 3"

different color strips of paper to write fortunes

scissors

stapler

imagination to write creative fortunes

cookies (optional)

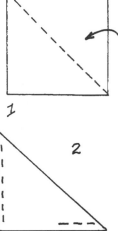

Preparation

Ask children to fold diagonal corners of the square together to form a triangle (1). Staple or glue the edges, leaving a portion open (2). Have children write a fortune on a strip of paper (3), fold the strip, and slip it into the triangle paper cookie (4).

Collect the cookies and mix them up for children to pick their fortune. You may want to suggest that fortune strips stick out of the pouch, so they are easier to find without tearing the pouch.

3

4

If you serve real cookies, arrange them on a serving plate, each with a paper fortune cookie underneath. When children take turns reaching for a cookie, they get a fortune, too.

Hug a Book

The following craft can fit with any book program.

Craft an *I Love Books* Card

Supplies

one sheet computer or construction paper per child
scissors
glue
art materials of your choice

Preparation

Prepare sample pattern sheets or have children create their own. This project has three components that will be glued together. The body portion is a 3-1/2" strip cut lengthwise from the paper. Direct children to write Books or the title of their favorite book in the center on one side and decorate around the words (1).

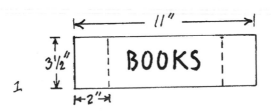

Boys and girls can use the remaining paper to cut hands and a head, which can be decorated as a self-portrait. Encourage children to add details, such as nails and rings, to the hands before gluing them and head to the body (2). Show children how to fold the body and hands into three sections. Have them write *I* on one outer side *Love* on the other to create their *I Love Books* hug-a-book card (3).

I Love Books Vest

What better way to declare a love of books than to wear the message!

Craft an I Love to Read Vest

Supplies

1 large paper grocery sack for each participant

scissors

art materials of your choice

Presentation

I hope you can find paper grocery bags. Our local grocery gives a choice of paper or plastic. Many of the bags I get have printing on them that takes away from any decorations. I have tried to turn them inside out, which works, but it might be easier to just cover the printing with a cut and glued construction paper design.

To make the sample vest, cut the bag up the middle (1). Cut a hole for the neck into the bottom part of the bag on which it stands (2). Cut armholes in each side of the bag (3). You may want to cut fringe across the bottom.

Decorate the outside with characters from a favorite book or an I Love to Read logo.

Read Pin

The wearer of this pin helps promote reading all day everyday. Therefore, encourage children to make more than one pin: one for themselves and one for a friend or relative.

Craft a Read Pin

Supplies

a plastic name tag holder for each pin

felt-tip pens

white glue

glitter

3" x 5" index cards for each pin

newspaper to cover the
      work area to
      catch excess glue
      and glitter

Preparation

Cover the crafters' work area with newspaper. Cut index cards to fit in the name tag holders.
    Ask each child to design a card with a reading logo of their choice. Offer felt-tip pens to color the cards. Then tell children to outline areas they want to decorate with glue. Help them sprinkle the wet areas with glitter, then shake off the excess glitter and glue.

When the glittery glue is dry, gently insert the card into the plastic name tag holder and show everyone how reading shines.

Hint: If plastic name tag holders are too expensive, tape safety pins to the back of the decorated index cards.

Resources

A Crafty Idea!

Charles Ghigna

Every craft you want to learn
Is found inside a book.
So step into your library
And take a crafty look!

There are always a number of craft books in print. You can usually find a large selection at the bookstore or library. If you are of "a certain age," as the French say, many of the crafts will have a dé-jà vu feel, but remember they are new to the children. I rather like the fact that there are traditional crafts that are passed from generation to generation.

Book about Craftspeople

Castaneda, Omar S. *Abuela's Weave*. Art by Enrique O. Sanchez. Lee and Low, 1993. A little girl and her grandmother take their weaving to a Guatemalan festival.

General

Bingham, Caroline, and Karen Foster, eds. *Crafts for Celebration*. Illustrated with photos. Millbrook, 1993. One in the Millbrook Arts Library series. Overview of folk crafts used in celebrations, with some directions for crafts: masks, corn dollies, hand painting.

Sattler, Helen Roney. *Recipes for Art and Craft Materials.* Lothrop, 1987. Instructions for making paste, papier-mâché, and paints.

Speicher, John, ed. *Reader's Digest Crafts and Hobbies.* Reader's Digest, 1979. Step-by-step photos show how to do a variety of crafts in a 450-page compendium.

Temko, Florence. *Animals and Birds.* Art by the author. Millbrook, 1995. One in a series of books that provide clear pictorial directions for easy-to-make crafts.

Periodicals

Crafts: Decorative and Applied Arts Magazine. Crafts Council. 44A Pentonvile Rd., London N19BY, England. Glossy oversized bimonthly that reviews and previews exhibitions and articles about artists.

Crafts Beautiful. Maze Media Castle House. 97 High St., Colchester, Essex CO11TH, England. Ideas for patchwork, cross stitch, rubber stamping, crochet, tin can, and dough crafts.

Handcraft Illustrated. 17 Station St., Brookline, MA 02146. Quarterly. Quick and easy projects plus more advanced ideas for crafters, such as stenciling, boxes, metal crafts, and mixed media.

Pop-Ups

Jackson, Paul. *The Pop-Up Book*. Art by the author. Holt, 1996. Techniques and designs for over 100 paper pop-up projects.

Valenta, Barbara. *Pop-O-Mania: How to Create Your Own Pop-Ups*. Art by the author. Dial, 1997. Directions are easy to understand because the examples are three-dimensional.

Resources for Adults

Earl-McEwen, Terri, and Jenni Hukme. *Discover Rubber Stamping*. Chartwell (Quintet), 1996. Ideas for decorating with rubber stamps.

Jackson, Paul. *The Art and Craft of Paper Sculpture*. Art by the author. Chilton, 1996. Basic and advanced techniques for paper sculpture.

Stevens, Clive. *Paper Craft School*. Photos and drawings. Quarto, Reader's Digest, 1996. Techniques for making a large variety of paper crafts, including weaving, origami, collage, and papier-mâché.

Welford, Lin. *The Art of Painting Animals on Rocks*. Art by the author. Northlight, 1994. Step-by-step ideas for acrylic painting on rocks.

Resources for Children

Caney, Steven. *Steven Caney's Kid's America*. Illustrated with drawings and photos. Workman, 1978. A large compilation of ideas and crafts from colonial times to the present.

Carlson, Laurie. *Kids Create!* Williamson, 1990. Sand castles, paper bag piñatas, and clay projects are all illustrated with line drawings.

Dondiego, Barbara L. *After-School Crafts for Kids.* Art by Jacqueline Cawley. TAB (McGraw-Hill), 1992. Crafts with everyday household items such as coffee filters, juice cans, eggs, and sand.

Healton, Sarah H., and Kay Healton Whiteside. *Me Too! Creative Crafts for Preschoolers.* TAB McGraw, 1992. Beanbags, macaroni beads, bird feeder, and puppet ideas.

Lehne, Judith Logan. *The Never-Be-Bored Book.* Art by Morissa Lipstein. Sterling, 1992. Quick things to do when there's nothing to do, such as make a paper fortune-teller, tube kazoo, and fling butterfly.

Milne, Lyndsay. *Fun Factory: Games and Toys from Household Junk.* Reader's Digest Kids, 1995. Colorful step-by-step drawings with hints for recycling, such as a paper clip yacht, stilts, and masks.

Reid, Margarette S. *A Ring of Beads.* Art by Ashley Wolff. Dutton, 1997. With a bit of history and some craft directions, this picture book is a worthwhile survey of beads.

Ruelle, Karen Gray. *75 Fun Things to Make and Do by Yourself.* Art by Sandy Haight. Sterling, 1995. Create a baking soda volcano, potato prints, and outdoor activities.

Treinen, Sara Jane, ed. *Incredibly Awesome Crafts for Kids.* Meredith Corporation, 1992. Sponge painting, torn paper crafts, card crafts, paper punch, dough, and felt projects.

Wiseman, Ann Sayre. *Making Things: The Handbook of Creative Discovery.* Art by the author. Little, 1997. Includes 125 projects to craft.

Origami

Kitamura, Keiji. *Origami Animals.* Kodansha (distributed by Farrar, Strauss), 1994. How to make charming paper animals step-by-step.

Montroll, John. *Prehistoric Origami: Dinosaurs and Other Creatures.* Dover, 1989. Patterns and directions for creating your favorite dinosaurs.

Tremaine, Jon. *The Amazing Book of Origami.* Art by the author. Colour Library (England), 1994. Clear color step-by-step drawings and photographs of hands demonstrating the folds for beginners to advanced origami makers.

Caroline Feller Bauer has traveled in more than one hundred countries, lecturing in more than sixty. She is well known around the world for her lively show-and-tell lectures to children, parents, and professionals in which she features creative ideas for bringing children and books together.

A member of the Puppeteers of America and the Miami Puppet Guild, she is the recipient of many awards. She is the author of the classic *Caroline Feller Bauer's New Handbook for Storytellers* (ALA, 1993), *Leading Kids to Books through Magic* (ALA, 1996), *Leading Kids to Books through Puppets* (ALA, 1997), and seventeen other books for children and adults.